D1180210

THREE PRESIDENTS AND THEIR BOOKS

fifth
annual
Windsor
Lectures

THREE PRESIDENTS

UNIVERSITY OF ILLINOIS PRESS, URBANA, 1955

THE READING OF

Jefferson / ARTHUR BESTOR

Lincoln / DAVID C. MEARNS

Franklin D. Roosevelt / JONATHAN DANIELS

AND THEIR BOOKS

THIRD PRINTING

 Manufactured in the United States of America. Library of Congress Catalog Card No. 54-12305.

FOREWORD

In the space of five years, the Windsor Lectures in Librarianship have become an institution on the University of Illinois campus. The series was inaugurated in 1949 by John T. Winterich, who spoke on the American booktrade for the fifty-year period 1876–1926. The following year, possible scientific solutions to problems created by the multiplication of scholarly materials were examined by Louis Ridenour, Ralph Shaw, and Albert Hill. Bibliographical aspects of nineteenth-century English books were discussed by Gordon Ray, Carl Weber, and John Carter, for the 1951 program; and in 1952, Harold Guinzburg, Theodore Waller, and Robert Frase considered various phases of current book publishing. All four series have been issued in handsome and appropriate formats by the University of Illinois Press.

The Windsor Lectureship was established by alumni of the University of Illinois Library School to honor Phineas Lawrence Windsor, who retired in 1940, after rounding out a distinguished career of thirty-one years as Director of the University Library and Library School. Under Professor Windsor's guidance and leadership, the Library School developed an outstanding faculty, a strong curriculum, and excellent physical facilities, while the Library gained a position in the forefront of American university libraries. The endowed lectureship created by several thousand alumni is an appropriate recognition of Professor Windsor's contributions to the library world.

The 1953 series of Windsor Lectures is concerned with books, of course, as were the first four, but the approach is quite different from those of 1949–1952. The broad central theme is "Books and American Statesmanship," or stated more explicitly, the influence of books and reading, insofar as it can be determined, on the minds, characters, personalities, and actions of three selected leaders in American political life. Such an assignment is filled with difficulties and pitfalls, admittedly, for who can measure with any degree of objectivity anything as intangible as the impact of reading on any individual? Nevertheless, through a person's expressed thoughts, the writers whom he is known to have admired and quoted, and other criteria, we may be able to surmise something of the effects of certain books on his intellectual development. That is the task which the three Windsor Lecturers for 1953 set themselves and attempted to explore.

These three men—Arthur Bestor, David Mearns, and Jonathan Daniels—have been in intimate touch with their subjects for long periods, through extended study, or, in the case of Mr. Daniels, by personal association. They bring exceptional qualifications, therefore, to their discussions. The three notables who were chosen for consideration—Jefferson, Lincoln, and Franklin Roosevelt—are known to have been bookmen, though in varying degrees and in different fashions. They are treated here in chronological order.

Arthur E. Bestor, Jr. is an alumnus of Yale, and has been on the history faculties at Yale, Columbia, Stanford, and, since 1947, the University of Illinois. The awards and honors which have come to him in the past twenty years make an impressive list. As a historian, he is primarily concerned with the American field. More specifically, his research, writing, and publishing have dealt with the intellectual history of the United States, and with communitarian socialism in America. His *Backwoods Utopias,* issued by the University of Pennsylvania Press in 1950, was widely and favorably reviewed. His newest book, *Educational Wastelands,* was published by the University of Illinois Press late in 1953, and since then has kept a ferment stirring in the educational world. Professor Bestor is presently engaged in writing an intellectual history of the United States, a field in which Thomas Jefferson naturally played a conspicuous part. Out of these investigations has come the basis for Professor Bestor's essay on "Thomas Jefferson and the Freedom of Books."

The second Windsor Lecturer, David C. Mearns, is one of the *rara avis,* a native of Washington, D.C., and has always lived in the Washington area. He joined the staff of the Library of Congress in 1918, and has served successively as a reference assistant, stack inspector, special assistant and chief assistant in the reading rooms, superintendent of the reading rooms, chief reference librarian, director of the reference department, and most recently as chief of the Manuscripts Division and assistant librarian for the American Collections. His versatile pen has produced *The Constitution of the United States, an Account of Its Travels; Magna Carta: the Lincoln Cathedral Copy; Lincoln Collections in the Library of Congress; The Story Up to Now* (a history of the Library of Congress); *The Lincoln Papers;* and *Jefferson's Other Seedling.* For a number of years, Mr. Mearns has specialized in Lincoln research, and he was the obvious person to be placed in charge of the opening of the celebrated Robert Todd Lincoln papers at the Library of Congress in 1947, at the end of the twenty-five year waiting period stipulated by the donor. His edition of the Lincoln papers, issued by Doubleday in 1948, was acclaimed by scholars.

In his study of Lincoln's reading, for the Windsor series, Mr. Mearns has made extensive use of original sources, hitherto not consulted. He has subjected the work of earlier writers to a critical analysis and contributed valuable new findings, to give us for the first time an accurate understanding of Lincoln's tastes in books and reading.

The final Windsor Lecturer for 1953 has had an extraordinarily varied career since he first saw the light of day in Raleigh, North Carolina. Essentially, however, he has always remained a newspaperman at heart, whatever else he might have been doing—as was his father before him. In his college days at the University of North Carolina, Jonathan Daniels became editor of the *Tar Heel*, the student newspaper. He and Tom Wolfe were contemporaries and friends at Chapel Hill. Through college, Mr. Daniels spent a year at the Columbia Law School and was later admitted to the North Carolina bar, but decided against a barrister's life and joined the *Louisville Times* as a reporter. In the years following, he served as Washington correspondent for his father's newspaper *The Raleigh News and Observer*, published a novel, *Clash of Angels*, traveled in Europe on a Guggenheim Fellowship, and was on the editorial staff of *Fortune* magazine. After his father became ambassador to Mexico, he took over editorship of *The News and Observer*, long one of the South's leading newspapers.

During the second World War, Mr. Daniels began a succession of responsible assignments: assistant director of the Office of Civilian Defense, 1942; administrative assistant to the president, 1943–45; and White House secretary in charge of press relations, 1945. Since the war, he has been a member of the UN Subcommittee on Prevention of Discrimination and Protection of Minorities, and of the ECA Public Administrative Board. He has now returned to the editorship of *The News and Observer*, but keeps his hand in the political arena by serving as Democratic National Committeeman from North Carolina.

In the midst of his diverse interests, Mr. Daniels has found time to wield a prolific pen. Among his best-known books are *A Southerner Discovers the South, A Southerner Discovers New England, Frontier on the Potomac,* and a biography of Harry Truman, *The Man of Independence,* which created considerable stir when it appeared in 1950.

In writing on "Franklin Delano Roosevelt and Books," Mr. Daniels brings firsthand knowledge. His acquaintance with FDR began as long ago as Woodrow Wilson's administration, when his father, Josephus Daniels, was secretary and Roosevelt was assistant secretary of the Navy. The relationship became much closer, of course, in the closing years of Roosevelt's life.

From these essays on three of our most famous presidents there emerge remarkable differences and occasional similarities in the roles which books played in their lives. It is apparent that Jefferson was the greatest bookman, and probably the most widely read of American presidents; Lincoln's reading was more intensive than extensive; while Roosevelt was an avid collector, a reader for recreation, and absorbed much knowledge of books indirectly through others. Having read the complete series, no one could question seriously the power and influence of the printed page on the intellectual growth of leaders whose impact on their times was doubtless greater than that of any other three individuals in American history.

ROBERT B. DOWNS
Director, Library and Library School
University of Illinois

CONTENTS

Thomas Jefferson and the Freedom of Books | 1
ARTHUR BESTOR

Mr. Lincoln and the Books He Read | 45
DAVID C. MEARNS

Franklin Delano Roosevelt and Books | 89
JONATHAN DANIELS

THOMAS JEFFERSON
AND THE FREEDOM OF BOOKS

BY ARTHUR BESTOR

Just at nightfall on the evening of Wednesday, August 24, 1814, a British force of some four thousand men camped at the eastern edge of Washington, D.C., having triumphed that afternoon over the poorly organized and wretchedly commanded defenses of the city. Within a few minutes the two wings of the Capitol (as yet unconnected by a central rotunda and dome) were wrapped in flames, ignited by order of the two British commanders, Major General Robert Ross and Rear Admiral Sir George Cockburn, who themselves attended personally to the firing of the White House later in the evening.[1] Dolly Madison managed to rescue the Cabinet papers, Gilbert Stuart's portrait of Washington, and some silverware and china from the White House, while a couple of clerks succeeded in removing a few cartloads of books and documents from the Capitol.[2] In the latter building, however, had been assembled some three thousand volumes to constitute "the library of the two Houses of

Congress," and the greater part of these went up in smoke.[3]

When the news reached Monticello, a hundred miles away, it found the seventy-one-year-old Thomas Jefferson occupied with plans for the projected University of Virginia. In the fury of the moment he suggested retaliation for the destruction at Washington. "We," he wrote, "can burn their St. James' and St. Paul's by means of our money, offered to their own incendiaries, of whom there are thousands in London who would do it rather than starve."[4] His second thought was more Jeffersonian. A month after the burning of the Capitol he wrote to President Madison reporting that he had already offered his own magnificent personal library to Congress for purchase at their own valuation. "I have long been sensible," he wrote, "that my library would be an interesting possession for the public, and the loss Congress has recently sustained, and the difficulty of replacing it, while our intercourse with Europe is so obstructed, renders this the proper moment for placing it at their service."[5]

The offer was accepted, but only after one of the most mean-spirited party battles in Congressional annals. Full-scale debate began in the House of Representatives on October 17, 1814, the very day on which the legislature of Massachusetts issued its call for the notorious Hartford Convention. It was resumed at various times until the end of the following January. The New England Federalists, bitterly hostile to "Mr. Madison's War," visited their wrath upon the hapless library of his predecessor and friend. Cyrus King of Massachusetts—half-brother of Rufus, and graduate of Columbia in the class of '94—was one who threw himself wholeheartedly into the battle to save the Republic from the menace of Jefferson's books. "It might be inferred," he said, "from the character of the man who collected it, and France, where the collection was made, that the library contained irreligious and immoral books, works of the French philosophers, who caused and influenced the volcano of the

French Revolution. . . . The bill would put $23,900 into Jefferson's pocket for about 6,000 books, good, bad, and indifferent, old, new, and worthless, in languages which many can not read, and most ought not." This, he concluded, "is true Jeffersonian, Madisonian philosophy, to bankrupt the Treasury, beggar the people, and disgrace the nation." [6]

The nation has borne the disgrace very well indeed. The Library of Congress is the living monument of this transaction of 1815, and in its rare book room are carefully preserved the two thousand volumes that still remain from Jefferson's original collection of six thousand. Surrounding this precious nucleus, in the reading rooms, the stacks, and the annex, are the millions of volumes that have subsequently been assembled in pursuance of Jefferson's principle of building democracy upon a foundation of vigorous, enlightened, fearless intellectual effort.

The library which became the property of the nation in 1815 was neither the first nor the last that Jefferson collected, and neither the first nor the last that he intended for public use. His earliest collection of books perished in the fire that destroyed his birthplace, Shadwell, in 1770.[7] The library that went to Congress was the fruit of forty-five years of collecting—in the bookshops of Europe, from the catalogues of dealers, through the gifts of authors whom he had assisted in their researches. But even as the last cases of books rolled off on wagons to Washington, Jefferson began assembling his third personal library,[8] which numbered nearly a thousand volumes at the time of his death eleven years later.[9]

As early as 1779, moreover, Jefferson drafted and presented to the Virginia General Assembly a Bill for Establishing a Public Library, wherein "the learned and curious" might carry on their researches "without fee or reward." [10] This project proved abortive, but Jefferson as president of the United States had a direct hand in planning and selecting the books for the earliest library established by Congress in the new Capitol.[11] The transfer of his own private library to the nation in 1815 was thus a continuation of services he had already grown accustomed to rendering. Another great library occupied the attention of his later years—that of the University of Virginia, of which he was the father in a more direct and inclusive sense than has been true of the founders of most institutions. The record of his devotion to the library of the new University is a manuscript list of over three thousand titles which he drew up with thoughtfulness, learning, and care to provide a basis for the purchases which the Board of Visitors had authorized.[12]

Jefferson's libraries were for use. He loved books, he chose editions with discrimination, he respected rarities, he paid attention to the proper binding of ephemera, he was careful of the physical condition of his volumes. But his ultimate purpose was not to display his library but to live with it and to make its volumes work for him and for others.

We owe much to this mating of the collector's instinct with the ideal of service to the state. An admirable example is the collection which Jefferson made of the early laws of Virginia. Eleven volumes of manuscript documents were eventually acquired by him—from the son of Sir John Randolph, who in the earlier eighteenth century "had collected papers with a view to write the history of Virginia"; [13] from the estates of other Virginians; from a pile of waste paper in a tavern, where parts of the records "had been already cut off for thread papers & other uses"; [14] from manuscripts which he could not acquire himself but which he laboriously transcribed in his own hand. The fugitive sheets of printed laws from 1734 onwards were likewise gathered and bound by Jefferson. Together with the more formal published volumes of Virginia statutes which he likewise possessed and arranged, these materials constituted the most complete and important body of sources on the legal and statutory history of the colony that survived into the nineteenth century. As early as 1796 Jefferson was corresponding with his old teacher George Wythe concerning publication of the complete documentary record.[15] When in 1806 William Waller Hening planned such a work, he wrote Jefferson that if he undertook it he would have to be, "in a great measure, dependent upon you for materials." Jefferson co-operated to the full, lending many of his volumes and superintending the transcribing of those that were too fragile to be transported. When Hening's *Statutes at Large; Being a Collection of All the Laws of Virginia* began to appear in 1809, Jefferson's contribution was fully recorded in preface, notes, and headings.[16] This did not bring to an end Jefferson's interest in the legal history of the colony where he was born. As a young lawyer, in the years from 1768 to 1772, he had taken down in writing the leading decisions of the General Court of Virginia. He had had access, moreover, to three manuscript volumes containing reports of cases decided between 1730 and 1740, and from these he had extracted "every case of domestic character." The value to posterity of these documents was as much in his mind as their immediate usefulness in his own legal practice. "As precedents," he explained in a preface that he wrote for the collection, "they established authoritatively the construction of our own enactments, and gave them the shape and meaning, under which our property has been ever since transmitted, and is regulated and held to this day." [17] Jefferson did not publish the materials himself, but the carefully preserved collection was put in print in 1829 as a regular volume of legal *Reports,* with Jefferson's name on the title page as reporter.

An active concern that the books and manuscripts he collected should be put to use was characteristic of Jefferson. Occasionally it led him into practices at which a bibliophile would shudder. Jefferson did not hesitate to take apart a sixteenth-century *editio princeps* of a Greek author, trim its margins to make it the size of a duodecimo instead of a quarto, interleave it with the pages of a seventeenth-century Latin translation, and bind up the whole in a series of small volumes for easier study and handling.[18] His purpose, however, was the far from vandalistic one of enabling him accurately to collate versions, even for purposes of personal correspondence.[19] And occasionally he indulged a satiric impulse, as when he bound up a group of scandalous court chronicles in a series labeled on the back "The Book of Kings." [20]

Usefulness was also the keynote of the classification scheme which Jefferson devised for his books, and which he worked over and refined to the end of his life. Significantly enough, he went to Sir Francis Bacon for the broad outline. This gave to his classification sufficient universality to permit it to be adopted by others and to influence library practice for close to a century.[21] Nevertheless Jefferson recognized—better than many who adopted his scheme—that classification depends largely on the use to which a library is to be put. "Thus," he wrote the librarian of Congress, "the law having been my profession, and politics the occupation to which the circumstances of the times . . . called my particular attention, my provision of books in these lines . . . was more copious, and required in particular instances subdivisions into sections and paragraphs, while other subjects of which general views only were contemplated are thrown into masses. A physician or theologist would have modified differently, the chapters, sections, and paragraphs of a library adapted to their particular pursuits." [22]

This statement authorizes us to look upon Jefferson's classification as, in some sense, a blueprint of his own mind. The emphasis or lack of emphasis which particular subjects received is a measure of the utility which Jefferson found in them. The relationships which his scheme established between different fields of knowledge are the relationships that Jefferson deemed significant in a practical or functional sense. A few of these emphases and relationships are worth noting.

Jefferson began with a threefold division of knowledge into History, Philosophy, and Fine Arts. This was justified, in Baconian terms, by analogy to three faculties of the mind: Memory, Reason, and Imagination. This somewhat quaint psychological explanation tends, however, to conceal the real meaning of the division. The first category, History, included natural history, and comprised in essence the *factual data* of every field of knowledge.[23] The second category, Philosophy, included mathematics, law, and politics, as well as ethics, and comprised in essence the *theoretical formulations* in every field.[24] That history should be linked with botany and disjoined from politics seems odd to us, accustomed as we are to such categories as natural sciences and social sciences. But Jefferson's scheme accurately reflected certain fundamental convictions of eighteenth-century philosophy: that experience provides all the raw material of thought; that laws in every field are arrived at by inductive reasoning from facts; and that scientific generalizations, ethical maxims, and political principles are at bottom mere manifestations of one universal and harmonious system which Jefferson could describe as "the Laws of Nature and of Nature's God."

The third and last of Jefferson's major categories, the Fine Arts, dramatizes the disjunction he instinctively felt between the useful and the beautiful. Fond though Jefferson might be of such arts as music and architecture, one cannot escape the impression that the third category was to him a distinctly inferior one. The classic works of literature whose subjects brought them within the rubrics of history or ethics were assigned immediately to these higher categories, leaving to the fine arts only those writings which were the product simply of "imagination."[25] Among the principles that Jefferson set down for the guidance of the University of Virginia one finds the austere pronouncement: "Nothing of mere amusement should lumber a public library." [26]

In the last analysis, books were tools, designed to assist men in the most serious and difficult of their labors. That these tools—especially the most useful and valuable of them—should be available to all was a first necessity in a republic. Jefferson emphasized this conception of the principal function of a library in the first of the "explanations" that he prefixed to the catalogue of books for the University of Virginia: "Great standard works of established reputation, too voluminous and too expensive for private libraries, should have a place in every public library, for the free resort of individuals." [27]

To make libraries available was, however, only part of the task. If books are to do their work, men must be guaranteed complete freedom of access to them. What Jefferson did to secure the freedom of books is a matter especially worthy of our attention in these troubled days of crisis and fear. To this subject I shall devote the remainder of my paper.

Censorship is, of course, the most direct way of denying men freedom of access to books and ideas, and censorship was abhorrent to Jefferson. "It is error alone which needs the support of government," he wrote in his *Notes on Virginia.* "Truth can stand by itself. Subject opinion to coercion: whom will you make your inquisitors? Fallible men; men governed by bad passions, by private as well as public reasons." [28] The issue did not remain a theoretical one. In 1814, only five months before Jefferson offered his personal library to Congress, he took up his pen in defense of a Philadelphia bookseller who was being prosecuted for selling a scientific work which the authorities deemed irreligious. "I am really mortified," wrote Jefferson, "to be told that, *in the United States of America,* a fact like this can become a subject of inquiry, and of criminal inquiry too . . . ; that a question about the sale of a book can be carried before the civil magistrate. . . . If M. de Bécourt's book be false in its facts, disprove them; if false in its reasoning, refute it. But, for God's sake, let us freely hear both sides, if we choose." [29]

In matters involving his own deepest interests Jefferson adhered to this principle. Despite the bitter hostility of the Federalist press during his presidency, he firmly stated his own conviction that the people "may safely be trusted to hear everything true and false, and to form a correct judgment between them." He considered liberty an experiment "which we trust will end in establishing the fact, that man may be governed by reason and truth. Our first object should therefore be, to leave open to him all the avenues of truth. The most effectual hitherto found, is the freedom of the press." [30]

As a public figure Jefferson was both co-operative and candid in furnishing information requested by numerous correspondents. His mission to France, in 1784–89, coincided with the first serious effort of Europeans to understand and assess the significance of the American Revolution. Jefferson himself printed and privately distributed his *Notes on Virginia* shortly after his arrival in Paris,[31] and thereafter till the end of his life he was consulted by almost every historian who undertook to narrate the rise of the new Republic. Jefferson gave all the assistance in his power to a succession of writers, reading their manuscripts, making corrections and offering suggestions, lending his own books, newspapers, and manuscripts, and even, at times, arranging for the printing or translating of new historical works.[32]

On every occasion Jefferson insisted that all the known facts should be told, whether or not they tended to support the cause or the position that he himself upheld. In Paris in 1786–87, for example, he furnished numerous memoranda and notes to the French historian François Soulés for use in his *Histoire des troubles de l'Amérique anglaise*. One passage of the book dealt with the raid of the British and Indians through the Wyoming Valley of Pennsylvania in 1778. After reading Soulés' draft, Jefferson discussed the event with J. Hector St. John de Crèvecoeur, procured documents which the latter had collected, and promptly forwarded them to the historian, in the full realization that the called-for revision would cause the narrative to "assume a different face, more favorable both to the British & Indians." [33]

Jefferson's own home at Monticello had been invaded by the British in June, 1781. Seven years later he was in correspondence with William Gordon, then engaged in writing a *History of the Rise, Progress, and Establishment, of the United States of America.* The question of the raid on Monticello came up. Jefferson insisted upon a strictly factual account. He described the devastation of his other plantation at Elkhill, but he refused to allow his resentment of this episode to color his narrative of the events at Monticello. To Gordon he wrote: "You ask, in your letter of Apr. 24. details of my sufferings by Colo[nel] Tarleton. I did not suffer by him. On the contrary he behaved very genteelly with me. On his approach to Charlottesville which is within 3. miles of my house at Monticello, he dispatched a troop of his horse under capt McLeod with the . . . object, of taking me prisoner with the two Speakers of the Senate & Delegates. . . . He gave strict orders to Capt McLeod to suffer nothing to be injured." Jefferson and his two colleagues in the government received warning in time to escape. "But," said Jefferson in concluding his narrative, "capt[ai]n McLeod preserved every thing with sacred care during about 18. hours that he remained there." [34]

In the years 1792–93, when Jefferson was secretary of state, he had the delicate task of providing from the confidential archives of the government the materials for a two-volume edition of *Official Letters to the Honorable American Congress, Written, During the War Between the United Colonies and Great Britain, by His Excellency, George*

Washington. The project originated with John Carey, who received permission to publish the work as a private venture. Jefferson devised a procedure for furnishing the documents requested, without giving the compiler access to the whole mass of confidential papers. He also examined the transcripts carefully, and referred to President Washington a few passages that might require continued secrecy. After the work was published Jefferson commented: "Tho' there were passages which might on publication create uneasiness in the minds of some, & were therefore referred by me to the President, yet I concurred fully in the opinion he pronounced that as these things were true they ought to be known. To render history what it ought to be the whole truth should be known. I am no friend to mystery & state secrets. They serve generally only to conceal the errors & rogueries of those who govern." [35]

Jefferson summarized his point of view in 1813, when he suggested the filling up of certain omissions in Thomas Clark's *Naval History of the United States.* "It is due to the honorable truths with which the book abounds," wrote Jefferson, "to publish those which are not so. A fair & honest narration of the bad is a voucher for the truth of what is good." [36]

Suppression of facts, of ideas, and of books belonged, in Jefferson's opinion, to the repressive systems of government from which the United States had declared their independence. In his own handling of controversial writings, he was true to the noble affirmation now engraved on the entablature of the Jefferson Memorial in Washington: "I have sworn upon the altar of god, eternal hostility against every form of tyranny over the mind of man." [37]

Now freedom of speech or opinion is a complicated matter. We do Jefferson an injustice if we quote merely his ringing affirmations of liberty without also observing how conscientiously he wrestled with the very real problems that a consistent defense of intellectual freedom involves. The believer in liberty, especially liberty of expression, faces an inescapable paradox. He must protect the right of other men to propagate ideas which he himself considers false and even perilous. This is difficult enough. But the shoe really begins to pinch when he finds himself obliged to tolerate, in the name of liberty, the circulation of writings that advocate the destruction of liberty. We are not the first to ask ourselves such questions as these: Can the right of free expression possibly extend to those who use it for the purpose of abolishing the right itself? Are we obliged to tolerate writings that seek to convert men to intolerance? Jefferson faced the same problems. We can learn a great deal, I believe, by observing how he undertook to defend liberty without curtailing the freedom to circulate books that are hostile to liberty.

At the outset, let us remember that we are concerned with the freedom of books and ideas. There is, after all, a distinction between ideas and overt acts. In practice the line is sometimes hard to draw, but the principle is clear. Men, of course, are always responsible before the law for their conduct. Riot, espionage, assassination, and treason are criminal offenses, whether the persons involved are impelled by idealism or suborned by bribery. But it is the act and not the idea for which they are punished. Thought must pass over the line into action—or must at least be poised at the very brink of overt action—before the law can meddle with it. Only when the expression of an idea is in some sense itself an act can even the *expression* become a matter of judicial attention. "The question in every case," according to the opinion which Mr. Justice Holmes wrote for a unanimous Supreme Court, "is whether the words used are used in such circumstances and are of such a nature as to create a clear and present danger that they will bring about the substantive evils that Congress has a right to prevent." [38] The law, in other words, is concerned with substantive evils, not with ideas in the abstract. I believe that Jefferson would have subscribed to Holmes's formulation of the doctrine of "clear and present danger," but this is not my present point. I am simply observing that Jefferson, in his discussions of freedom, made the elementary distinction that any logical thinker must make, between the expression of an idea and overt action based upon it.

There is an even more important and even more frequently forgotten distinction to bear in mind. Jefferson was completely free of one particular brand of intellectual confusion which is rife at the present day and which frequently paralyzes the defense of freedom. To explain it let me take as my text a familiar statement from Jefferson's First Inaugural Address: "If there be any among us who would wish to dissolve this Union or to change its republican form, let them stand undisturbed as monuments of the safety with which error of opinion may be tolerated where reason is left free to combat it." [39] This, be it observed, is a proclamation of *toleration* not of *neutrality*. There is no hint here of the muddle-headed notion that if a man has convictions he cannot allow himself to be tolerant, or if he is tolerant he cannot allow himself to take a stand on the issues involved. Jefferson speaks frankly and unabashedly of truth and error, and he uses the language of battle to describe the choice which thinking men must make between them: "Error of opinion may be tolerated where reason is left free to *combat* it."

Tolerance of dissenting opinions does not imply indifference to the issues presented. Throughout his long life Jefferson fought for the ideas he believed in. For some things he campaigned harder than for others, of course, but one can scarcely find a single live issue of his generation—from foreign policy to domestic slavery—on which he remained neutral. In fighting these battles of ideas, moreover, he brought into action every resource that he could command of reason, impassioned eloquence, legal argument, and political organization. That is to say, he wielded effectively all the weapons of controversy that men have ever deemed legitimate and honorable—all, that is, save one. He abjured completely the right to *suppress* an opposing idea. This self-denying ordinance, he believed, was a fundamental law of intellectual liberty. But it was the only self-denying ordinance he recognized in the matter.

Jefferson knew, and we ought to remember, that freedom of expression bestows upon an idea no immunity whatever from criticism. It restrains no man from wholehearted commitment to the principles he deems right and just. In point of fact, liberty requires of him just such a positive commitment. The defender of freedom must insist that no facts be suppressed and no opinions denied a hearing. But this is only half—and in a sense the negative half—of his obligation. He must also enlist in the affirmative battle for freedom. He must allow the forces of obscurantism and tyranny to speak their piece, but he must stand up himself and be counted in favor of reason and liberty. Jefferson did so, not only in his public life but in the privacy of his library. This is easy to say. But what, exactly, does positive commitment to the cause of freedom really mean when applied to a man's handling of books? A few illustrative episodes will give us Jefferson's answer.

Three great and influential books of the eighteenth century interested Jefferson and yet disturbed him. One was Montesquieu's *Spirit of Laws,* another was David Hume's *History of England,* the third was Blackstone's *Commentaries on the Laws of England.* Each was a masterpiece of its kind. Each conveyed ideas of the greatest importance and value. Each was in Jefferson's library and each was carefully studied by him. There could be no question of denying these books their rightful place in the making of American opinion. On the other hand, each work incorporated doctrines which Jefferson felt to be inimical to the ideals in which he believed and on which he felt the Republic to be founded. The fact that he respected these books was no reason for allowing their influence to go unchallenged. How Jefferson dealt with each of the three books illustrates his conception of the positive obligation of a believer in liberty.

Jefferson's opinion of Montesquieu was decidedly mixed. The *Spirit of Laws,* he wrote in 1790, "contains indeed a great number of political truths; but almost an equal number of political heresies: so that the reader must be constantly on his guard." [40] Jefferson seems not to have been bothered by the heresies in his first study of the work, for on the eve of the American Revolution he filled twenty-eight pages of his Commonplace Book with extracts from Montesquieu,[41] extracts which bolstered the very ideas that Jefferson was contending for. The change in attitude came after the Revolution was over, when Montesquieu's reverence for the British constitution began to appear to Jefferson altogether too Hamiltonian, and Montesquieu's misgivings about the possible excesses of democracy too likely to undermine faith in the government which the Americans had established for themselves.

In any case Jefferson began to include warnings against the "inconsistences, apocryphal facts, & false inferences" of the *Spirit of Laws,*[42] whenever he recommended the book for study. He began, moreover, to cast about for an antidote. One finally came to hand in 1809 in the form of a French critique by Count Destutt de Tracy. The author sent it to Jefferson with the request that it be translated and published anonymously in America. Jefferson promptly made the necessary arrangements, undertaking himself to revise and correct the translation.[43] Thereafter he earnestly recommended this *Commentary and Review of Montesquieu's Spirit of Laws* as "the elementary work for the youth of our academies and Colleges." [44] He was successful in securing its adoption at William and Mary,[45] and when at last a French edition appeared with the author's name, a copy was lodged cheek by jowl with the set of Montesquieu's works in the library of the new University of Virginia.[46]

Here, in its simplest form, was Jefferson's prescription for dealing with books which threatened to undermine certain principles that he deemed fundamental: *Permit the books to circulate freely, but encourage the most searching criticism of them and work vigorously to bring the criticisms to public attention.*

Jefferson ran into unparalleled difficulties in trying to counteract in the same way the influence of David Hume's *History of England.* He had to admit the superb literary qualities which made Hume "probably the most widely read and most influential of English historians" for the better part of a century following the publication of his work in the years 1754–62.[47] Jefferson's praise, indeed, was extravagant: "The charms of it's stile and selection of it's matter, had it but candor and freedom from political bias, would make it the most perfect sample of fine history which has ever flowed from the pen of man; not meaning to except even the most approved models of antiquity." [48] But the political bias was there and it was, of course, a Tory bias, completely intolerable to Jefferson. Hume's treatment of the seventeenth century seemed to Jefferson simply an *apologia* for the Stuart monarchs. "Their good deeds were displayed their bad ones disguised or explained away," he observed, ". . . and a constant vein of fine ridicule was employed to disparage the patriots who opposed their usurpations, and vindicated the freedom and rights of their country." [49]

It was the very virtues of Hume's style which made his book so menacing to republicanism. "I remember well," wrote Jefferson in 1810, "the enthusiasm with which I devoured it when young, and the length of time, the research

& reflection which were necessary to eradicate the poison it had instilled into my mind." [50] He concluded that "the young reader who can lay down Hume under any impression favorable to English liberty, must have a mind of extraordinary vigor and self possession." At times Hume loomed up as the most powerful and malevolent influence in modern politics. "What could not have been atchieved for the crown by any standing army, but with torrents of blood, one man, by the magic of his pen, has effected covertly, insensibly, peaceably," wrote Jefferson.[51] "It is this book which has undermined the free principles of the English government, has persuaded readers of all classes that these were usurpations on the legitimate and salutary rights of the crown, and has spread universal toryism over the land." [52] Nor was the United States safe from this baneful influence. Jefferson never doubted that sound knowledge of English history was essential to intelligent American citizenship. Our institutions, he wrote, "are so deeply laid in English foundations, that we shall never cease to consider their history as a part of ours and to study ours in that as it's origin." [53] But if a young reader learned his English history from Hume, Jefferson feared, he would grow up to be "the tory of our constitution, disposed to monarchise the government, by strengthening the Executive, and weakening the popular branch." [54]

From Jefferson's point of view this was indeed infiltration, boring from within, subversion, or what modern phrase you will. And Jefferson searched hard for some method of counteracting Hume's influence. His most ambitious proposal was addressed to the publisher Mathew Carey. "Reprint Hume with the text entire," he suggested, "and in collateral columns, or in Notes, place the Antidotes of it's disguises, it's misrepresentations, it's concealments, it's sophisms, and ironies; by confronting with them authentic truths from Fox, Ludlow, [Mrs. Catharine] McCaulay, Rapin and other honest writers." [55] A variorum edition of this kind would have constituted a sound scholarly enterprise, but no historian was prepared to carry it out, and no publisher was ready to gamble on it as a commercial venture.

Faced with so apparently hopeless a situation, Jefferson fell back upon an exceedingly dubious expedient. In the last years of the eighteenth century a certain John Baxter, ardent English liberal and constitutional reformer, began the publication of *A New and Impartial History of England, from the Most Early Period . . . to the Present Important and Alarming Crisis.* Originally issued in parts, the work was completed about 1796 as a quarto of more than eight hundred pages.[56] Jefferson seems to have discovered the book in 1805, and thereafter he tried to promote its use as a substitute for Hume. Baxter's method, as Jefferson described it, was one to make a scholar's hair stand on end. Baxter, he said, "gives you the text of Hume, purely and verbally, till he comes to some misrepresentation or omission, . . . he then alters the text silently, makes it what truth and candor say it should be, and resumes the original text again, as soon as it becomes innocent, without having warned you of your rescue from misguidance. And these corrections are so cautiously introduced that you are rarely sensible of the momentary change of your guide. You go on reading true history as if Hume himself had given it." [57]

It is embarrassing, to say the least, to find Jefferson recommending such a sorry combination of plagiarism, expurgation, and clandestine emendation. Little can be said in excuse. Jefferson, it is true, was thinking of a school text, and expurgation has, by long usage, become almost respectable in preparing books for the young. Moreover, Baxter did not actually try to trade on the reputation of Hume, for nowhere did he himself suggest that his history was an adaptation of the latter's. On the contrary he indicated his own political predilections in unmistakable fashion on the title page, which read: "By John Baxter, Member of the London Corresponding Society, and One of the Twelve Indicted and Acquitted of High Treason at the Old Bailey. Assisted by Several Gentlemen, Distinguished Friends to Liberty and a Parliamentary Reform." [58] The fact that Baxter himself did not sail under false colors, however, only makes Jefferson's conduct the more inexplicable, for the latter thought it would have been justifiable to use the title *Hume's History of England Abridged and Rendered Faithful to Fact and Principle.*[59] This would have been deliberate misrepresentation, whereas Baxter was guilty, at worst, of plagiarism—a rather venial sin to the tribe of Grub-Street writers who eked out a living by compiling popular histories in the eighteenth century.

All in all, Jefferson's effort to popularize Baxter must be regarded as one of his very few lapses—perhaps his only real lapse—from strict scholarly integrity. Fortunately the effort was dismally unsuccessful. Thrice Jefferson tried to induce an American publisher to reprint the work, and each time he failed—first with William Duane in 1810, next with Mathew Carey in 1818, and finally with Thomas W. White in 1820.[60] Jefferson was unable even to purchase a copy of Baxter's work to replace the one that went with the rest of his collection to the Library of Congress in 1815. He was still trying two years before his death, but even in London the work could not be procured.[61] And when the University of Virginia Library was finally put in order after Jefferson's death, the work of Baxter (which he once hoped might become a textbook there) was not to be found on its shelves.[62]

In the end, Jefferson turned to what was really the best answer of all: wider reading and more extensive knowledge. He urged visitors and correspondents to go back to the old *Histoire d'Angleterre* by Paul de Rapin Thoyras.[63] For the course of historical reading at the University of Virginia, he recommended beginning with Rapin's work as the most "faithful," and continuing, in succession, with the *Memoirs* of the seventeenth-century regicide General Edmund Ludlow, the vehemently anti-Tory *History of the Early Part of the Reign of James the Second* by Charles James Fox, and the voluminous writings of the Whig historian William Belsham. Thus suitably forewarned and forearmed, students might at last be introduced to Hume. Even then, however, they should be required to read at the same time George Brodie's newly published *History of the British Empire,* which dealt "unanswerably" (so Jefferson thought) with some of Hume's misrepresentations. In his letter of advice concerning the University, Jefferson emphasized his point that "Hume, with Brodie, should be the last histories of England to be read. If first read, Hume makes an English tory, from whence it is an easy step to American toryism." [64]

Despite the painful episode of Baxter, Jefferson's final prescription for dealing with books like Hume's was as clear as his prescription with respect to Montesquieu, though somewhat different: *Permit the books to circulate freely, but encourage men to read so widely that they will not be intoxicated by the style or misled by the errors of any one book.*

Sir William Blackstone was another giant with whom Jefferson engaged in posthumous intellectual combat. The first volume of Blackstone's great *Commentaries on the Laws of England* was published in 1765, three years after Jefferson commenced the study of law with George Wythe at Williamsburg, and two years before he was admitted to the bar. The final volume appeared in 1769, the year Jefferson began his political career as a member of the Virginia House of Burgesses.[65] Jefferson recognized that Blackstone's was "the most elegant & best digested" of all the legal compendiums. But Jefferson believed that mastery of the law could be attained only through careful study of the cases, and his own scholarly legal training made him suspicious of all mere digests. When Jefferson surveyed the profession of law half a century after his own studies began, he attributed much of "the degeneracy of legal science" to the misuse of Blackstone. "A student finds there a smattering of every thing, and his indolence easily persuades him that if he understands that book, he is master of the whole body of the law. The distinction between these, & those who have drawn their stores from the deep and rich mines of Coke [on] Littleton, seems well understood even by the unlettered common people, who apply the appellation of Blackstone lawyers to these Ephemeral insects of the law." [66]

Superficiality in legal learning was bad enough, but Jefferson apprehended even more dangerous consequences from too steady a diet of Blackstone. The *Commentaries* presented English law as it was on the eve of the American Revolution, and Jefferson felt that the repressive tendencies which produced that conflict had subtly influenced the contemporaneous development of the law. He even coupled Blackstone with Hume, charging in 1814 that these two were "making tories" of the younger generation of Americans.[67] Twelve years later, with the new University of Virginia in his mind, Jefferson confided his misgivings more fully to Madison:

> You will recollect that before the revolution, Coke [on] Littleton was the universal elementary book of law students, and a sounder whig never wrote, nor of profounder learning in the orthodox doctrines of the British constitution, or in what were called English liberties. You remember also that our lawyers were then all whigs. But when his black-letter text, and uncouth but cunning learning got out of fashion, and the honied Mansfieldism of Blackstone became the student's hornbook, from that moment, that profession (the nursery of our Congress) began to slide into toryism, and nearly all the young brood of lawyers now are of that hue. They suppose themselves, indeed, to be whigs, because they no longer know what whigism or republicanism means.[68]

To safeguard liberty, nothing would do but to "uncanonise Blackstone" [69] and go back to the earlier and purer sources of the law. This was, in fact, the guiding principle of Jefferson's activities in the realm of jurisprudence throughout his life. Two months after the Declaration of Independence, it will be recalled, Jefferson withdrew from the Continental Congress to serve in the House of Delegates of his native state. From that time until 1779 he was deeply engaged, with his old teacher Wythe and with Edmund Pendleton, in drafting a complete revision of the laws in effect in Virginia, including the laws inherited from England. Jefferson went back to Bracton and to the Anglo-Saxon codes, and reported with "great satisfaction" that he "had only to reduce the law to it's antient Saxon condition, stripping it of all the innovations & rigorisms of subsequent times, to make it what it should be." [70]

This was, of course, a conscious exaggeration. As preceding quotations have shown, Jefferson's real hero was Sir Edward Coke. The author of the Declaration of Independence naturally sympathized with the great Chief Justice who challenged the royal prerogative and championed the Parliamentary cause in the struggles of the early seventeenth century. But this harmony of views merely enhanced the respect which Jefferson felt for Coke's legal learning. He was but expressing the considered judgment of virtually every student of the common law when he described Coke's *Institutes of the Laws of England* as "a perfect Digest of the Law as it stood in his day." [71]

The date of Coke's work, moreover, had peculiar significance for Americans. The first part of the *Institutes* was published in 1628, nine years after the convening of the earliest legislative body in the New World, the General Assembly of Virginia, and two years before the first meeting in America of the Great and General Court of the Massachusetts Bay Company. According to Jefferson's constitutional theory, the colonies ceased to be bound by statutory alterations made by the Parliament at Westminster, once their own legislatures began to function. Hence the treatise of Sir Edward Coke presented the law as it stood just before English and American concepts and practices began to diverge.[72] It followed from this that American lawyers should start their studies with Coke's *Institutes* and should trace the subsequent development of the law through the actual cases, carefully discriminating such principles as clearly belonged to the ancient common law from those that ought to be regarded as innovations introduced by English statutes or by the interpretations of English courts. Such a plan of legal reading was precisely what Jefferson recommended to young students throughout his life. The starting point was always Coke on Littleton. Subsequent reading was in the reports or abridgments, from Coke to the present. And Blackstone was set aside—precisely as Hume was set aside in the field of history—to be read as the very last book of all.[73]

Jefferson's insistence upon going back to "the real fountains of the law"[74] led to several corollary activities in the realm of books. It was a major reason for his interest in the Anglo-Saxon language and for his zeal to introduce the study of that subject into the curriculum of the University of Virginia.[75] Jefferson was also anxious for the great classics of the English law to be made more available, and he urged Dr. Thomas Cooper to produce an English translation of Henry de Bracton's *De Legibus et Consuetudinibus Angliae*, reminding him that the work was written "a very few years after Magna Charta" and thus at the very point at which the common law began to be supplemented by statutes.[76] At the same time Jefferson proposed two other projects, both of which would have emphasized the historical sources of the law. One was for a work that would take up the doctrines of Bracton one by one and trace the history of each "thro' the periods of L[or]d Coke and [Matthew] Bacon, down to Blackstone."[77] The other was for an annotated edition of Blackstone, which would digest the cases (particularly the eighteenth-century cases) upon which Blackstone's pronouncements rested.[78]

In the realm of the law Jefferson was even more thoroughly the scholar than in the realms of political philosophy and history. His prescription for dealing with ideas which he disapproved or distrusted in this field was the most clear-cut of all his prescriptions, and it is precisely that which every real scholar would make: *Permit the books containing these ideas to circulate freely, but direct men constantly back to the original sources, so that they can weigh for themselves the evidence behind every conclusion.*

At the outset of this discussion of Montesquieu, Hume, and Blackstone, the question was raised: What, exactly, does positive commitment to the cause of freedom really mean when applied to a man's handling of books? Jefferson's answer, as these three instances have shown, was a positive not a negative one. The believer in freedom must not attempt to make his ideas prevail by suppressing or censoring or impeding the circulation of writings with which he disagrees. In his defense of liberty he must be faithful to the method of liberty. He must maintain a free marketplace of ideas. But his responsibility does not stop with this. He must bring to that marketplace the ideas he believes in. He must state his own doctrines affirmatively. He must fearlessly expose the errors and criticize the opinions of those with whom he disagrees. He must urge men to read widely and study deeply, so that knowledge and reason, rather than ignorance and prejudice, may form their opinions and govern their actions.

Jefferson applied similar principles to the realm of education, that is, to the problem of academic freedom. On March 4, 1825, just three days before the first classes actually met at the new University of Virginia, the Board of Visitors of the institution convened at Charlottesville. Despite his eighty-one years, Jefferson, the rector of the University, was an active participant in the deliberations. A month earlier he had been turning over in his mind the question of what responsibility the governing body should take for the political philosophy to be expounded in the classrooms of the University. He concluded that the issues of government were of such importance "as to make it a duty in us, to lay down the principles which are to be taught." Accordingly Jefferson drafted a resolution on the subject and submitted it to certain of his colleagues on the board, including James Madison. The latter made a number of suggestions, which Jefferson incorporated, and the revised resolution was formally adopted by the Visitors at their meeting of March 4, 1825.[79]

The preamble declared that the board had a "duty" to the state and nation "to pay especial attention to the principles of government which shall be inculcated" in the University, "and to provide that none shall be inculcated which are incompatible with those on which the Constitutions of this state and of the U[nited] S[tates] were genuinely based, in the common opinion." The preamble concluded with the following words: "For this purpose it may be necessary to point out specifically where these principles are to be found legitimately developed."

The resolution proper was in two parts. The first simply offered a list of six books or documents which, in the opinion of the Board of Visitors, stated the underlying principles of government in a form "generally approved by our fellow-citizens." The first two titles were John Locke's *Essay Concerning the True Original, Extent, and End of Civil Government*, and Algernon Sidney's *Discourses concerning Government*, which were recommended for their treatment of "the general principles of liberty and the rights of man." The remaining four were described as the "best guides" to "the distinctive principles of the government of our own state, and of that of the U[nited] S[tates]." Each document was accompanied by a brief comment, indicating the reasons for selecting it. First was the Declaration of Independence, included because it was "the fundamental act of union of these states." Following this was *The Federalist,* "being an authority to which appeal is habitually made by all . . . as evidence of the general opinion of those who framed, and of those who accepted the Constitution of the U[nited] S[tates] on questions as to it's genuine meaning." Next among the recommended texts were the so-called Virginia Resolutions of 1798 together with related resolutions and reports of 1799 and 1800. These documents, which were drafted by Madison and adopted by the General Assembly of Virginia, protested against the Alien and Sedition Acts of the Federalist Administration, and developed in notable form the twin doctrines of states' rights and of strict construction of the Constitution. The inclusion of the Resolutions of 1798 was justified by the Board of Visitors on the ground that they "appeared to accord with the predominant sense of the people of the U[nited] S[tates]." The final document on the list was George Washington's Farewell Address, which, in the words of the board, conveyed "political lessons of peculiar value."

The last section of the resolution contained the only strictly mandatory provision, and it applied to only one branch of a single one of the eight schools into which the University of Virginia was organized. The wording was as follows: "And that in the branch of the school of Law, which is to treat on the subject of Civil polity, these [i.e., the works previously listed] shall be used as the text and documents of the school."

In the eyes of many, this has seemed an extraordinary document to have come from the pen of Jefferson. Several of his best-informed admirers have simply passed it by without comment, thus mutely indicating their disapproval. The two ablest historians of the University of Virginia have been frankly critical. Herbert Baxter Adams, writing in 1888, condemned as "intolerable" the imposition of "a permanent educational or party yoke," which could only result in "narrowing political science to a party platform." [80] In similar vein, Philip Alexander Bruce, writing in 1920, adjudged Jefferson's action to be "inconsistent with the general character of independence which he endeavored so sedulously and so successfully to stamp upon the institution." The resolution meant, said Bruce, that the school of law, "instead of teaching the Federalist and Republican respective views of the National Government on a footing of historical and academic equality," was required to "put its emphatic *imprimatur* upon the Republican theory." Consequently the resolution gave the University "a definite bias, from a purely party point of view, from the start." [81]

These are weighty objections. The evidence, moreover, definitely shows that the matter uppermost in Jefferson's mind was his fear lest the professor of law still to be appointed might be "too much infected with the principles of the Richmond lawyers, who are rank Federalists as formerly denominated, & now Consolidationists." [82] Without question the Virginia Resolutions of 1798 were included in the list to uphold the states'-rights, strict-constructionist interpretation of the Constitution. Madison, indeed, was keenly aware of the danger that certain aspects of the proposal "might excite prejudices against the University as under party Banners." [83] The action of the Board of Visitors does point up, in unmistakable fashion, the very real perils that lurk in any measure dealing with political loyalty—perils that arise from the inescapable human tendency to confuse loyalty to the Constitution with loyalty to one's own particular interpretation of it.

On the whole, however, the partisan aspects of the University action have been overemphasized in most discussions. Only one of the six documents in the list—the Virginia Resolutions of 1798—reflected in any way the strictly *party* position of Jefferson and Madison. Other listed writings—

such as the *Federalist* papers and Washington's Farewell Address—certainly gave adequate representation to the tendencies in American political thinking that pointed in a different, or even opposite, direction. Taken as a whole, the list was a fair and balanced presentation of the range of political philosophies that actually entered into the making of our constitutional system. The states'-rights, strict-constructionist position was fully entitled to representation in such a list, and the Virginia Resolutions of 1798 constituted the most eligible and impressive statement of that position. They derived their authority not from Madison's authorship but from the fact that they were passed and subsequently reaffirmed by the General Assembly of the state that was establishing and supporting the University. Though the Resolutions of 1798 may be termed a party document, such a description is misleading, for they were, in fact, an elaborate defense of freedom of speech, of the press, and of religion, based on the argument that the Constitution in general and the First Amendment in particular forbade the federal government to intrude upon this sphere of reserved rights.[84]

Once Jefferson's inclusion of the Virginia Resolutions of 1798 is placed in proper perspective, certain substantial merits of his proposal of 1825 for the University begin to appear. To be accurate, I should refer to it as the proposal of Jefferson and Madison, for many salutary features were the result of the latter's suggestions, which Jefferson adopted.[85] The measure, let me remind you, was concerned with loyalty, and it undertook to handle the problem within the context of academic freedom. The procedure devised is worthy of our respectful attention if only because it represents the considered judgment of two of our most unmistakably liberal presidents. In point of fact it deserves attention on its merits, for this all-but-forgotten resolution of 1825 seems to me to point out a safe, effective, affirmative approach to the question of loyalty, an approach both applicable and desirable at the present hour, when so many dubious measures are in vogue.

Jefferson and Madison believed that the governing body of an educational institution possessed the right to impose standards of political and constitutional loyalty upon its faculty. They not only believed in the right, they actually exercised it. Madison recognized that they were "framing a political creed," and he was aware that there was some resemblance to the kind of religious test which both he and Jefferson repudiated. Madison insisted, however, that the "public right" was "very different in the two cases." [86] This distinction rested, of course, upon the constitutional separation of church and state. The state had no right to prefer one set of religious principles over another, for religious questions were constitutionally *ultra vires*. The state, however, was founded on one set of political principles, to the necessary exclusion of opposite principles, hence its concern that one set should prevail over the other was natural and proper. The major assumption of Jefferson and Madison—that standards of political and constitutional loyalty do not in themselves violate the principle of academic freedom—is unquestionably the assumption made today by public opinion and by the majority of agencies and associations concerned with academic policy. It is, in my judgment, a valid assumption. Requirements with respect to loyalty are in themselves perfectly compatible with academic freedom, provided they are established and applied in the same spirit and according to the same procedures that govern the establishment of other standards affecting the teaching profession. Let me argue this point in a brief digression.

A university is great in proportion to the intellectual freedom which its faculty and its students enjoy. This I hold as a self-evident truth. Freedom, however, cannot be defined in absolute terms apart from its context. In the realm of ideas, so it seems to me, there are at least three distinguishable forms of freedom, which can be described by the phrases: freedom of research or investigation, freedom of speech or publication, and freedom of teaching. These three freedoms have much in common, but they are not identical. Freedom of research is, almost necessarily, more far-reaching than freedom of publication. The laws of libel, for example, do not limit free investigation, but they properly limit free publication of the results of certain kinds of investigation. Likewise, freedom of speech or publication is more far-reaching than freedom of teaching. Lest this seem a doctrine weakening to the cause of liberty, let me offer one illustration not too highly charged with emotion. To prosecute a newspaper for publishing horoscopes would, I think, be an unwarranted invasion of the freedom of the press. On the other hand, I do not consider that freedom of teaching is jeopardized because no governing body of a reputable institution today would permit the offering of a course in astrology. In other words, a restriction which, if applied to investigation or publication, would constitute a grave infringement of liberty may not necessarily be a limitation of freedom at all if applied to formal instruction in the classroom. Academic freedom, it seems to me, requires a defense of all three kinds of freedom, each in its own terms. To confuse the three is to weaken the argument for each particular one.

Freedom of *teaching* is not necessarily curtailed because certain things are required to be taught in accordance with certain principles. A modern university would not become a place of greater intellectual freedom if it appointed an instructor in geography who, bowing to some private intuition, should insist upon teaching that the world is flat. Its very reputation as a great, and indeed a *free*, university depends upon its requiring that the various disciplines be taught in strict accord with the recognized principles and standards of each. Clearly there is no place in the classroom for a teacher of chemistry who expounds theories that chemists as a group would consider nonsense, for a teacher of mathematics who inculcates methods of reasoning that mathematicians would deem fallacious, for a teacher of history who offers interpretations that historians would find completely at variance with the evidence. The simple fact is that certain standards of intellectual conformity—the phrase is a disagreeable one, I know, but I repeat it—certain standards of intellectual conformity must necessarily be imposed upon the process of teaching, as a guarantee of professional integrity and responsibility. The freedom which the teaching profession must fight to retain is precisely the same kind of freedom that every other profession must fight to retain—not freedom from requirements and controls, but freedom from controls imposed by men ignorant of how research is conducted, and freedom from requirements that hamstring the profession in its legitimate work.

My purpose in saying all this is not to make us less vigilant in defending academic freedom, but to make our vigilance more effective by directing it upon the really crucial issue. This issue, as I see it, is not the existence of prescribed standards, but their nature, and the procedures used in enforcing them. What, then, are the characteristics which a set of requirements or standards should possess in order that they may insure the integrity of a profession without interfering with the freedom that is essential to its effective practice? If we examine carefully the nature of the standards by which academic competence is determined in matters other than loyalty, I think we can easily discover the answer.

The customary standards for determining academic competence are perfectly compatible with freedom of teaching because they prescribe not the specific conclusions to be taught but simply the forms of reasoning that may legitimately be used in reaching conclusions. One illustration should make this clear. As a historian my freedom is not hampered in the slightest way by the requirement that my conclusions must be supported by evidence and justified by logic. If, however, I am required willy-nilly to teach that an event happened in a particular way—that the American Revolution, for instance, was "caused" by certain factors specified for me—then I am utterly paralyzed as a historian. I am forbidden to employ whatever knowledge, skill, and powers of mind I may have in my own field, and I become simply a ventriloquist's dummy. The conclusion seems clear: If academic life is to be free and therefore fruitful, the standards controlling it must be of such a character as to permit the free play of intelligence, the free pursuit of originality, and the free exercise of critical responsibility.

The resolution which Jefferson and Madison drew up for the University of Virginia in 1825 seems to me to fulfill this condition. Despite their inclusion of the Virginia Document of 1798, they do not, in fact, fix a narrow standard of political orthodoxy. The resolution forbids, it is true, the inculcation of principles "incompatible with those on which the [state and federal] Constitutions . . . were genuinely based." But it recognizes that these principles comprise a diversity of political, constitutional, and social ideas. And it does not suggest that any one of these principles is to take precedence over the others in determining the standard of political loyalty.

The Constitution of the United States, after all, incorporates ideas from many different sources, it came into being as the result of numerous compromises, and it created what both Jefferson and Madison would have described as "mixed" governments. The state constitutions, moreover, vary from one another. The University resolution implicitly recognizes this fact of diversity by placing its stamp of approval on books representing an extremely wide range of political doctrine. Jefferson's great opponent Alexander Hamilton, it must be remembered, contributed the largest group of essays to

The Federalist, and one of his papers (the eighty-fourth) argued that it would be dangerous to append a Bill of Rights to the proposed Constitution. The Virginia Resolutions of 1798, by contrast, treated the Bill of Rights as the *sine qua non* of American constitutionalism. Other equally divergent points of view are to be found in the works approved by the Board of Visitors.

Far from inhibiting the free play of ideas, the books recommended could hardly fail to encourage it. They were not cut-and-dried manuals, but documents of controversy and argument, designedly written to encourage reasoned discussion. Only the most literal-minded pedagogue could possibly convert them into agents for stifling free speculation on the principles of government. When Jefferson prescribed them "as the text and documents" for the courses in civil polity, he certainly did not intend to make them the basis for an authoritarian kind of teaching, alien both to the spirit of the books themselves and to his own conception of what a university should be. He used the word "text," not so much in its modern meaning of handbook or manual, as in its ancient sense, which emphasized the distinction between the text, or original document, and the commentaries based upon it. From what we can gather of his ideas on instruction, Jefferson envisaged a course in which these texts would be carefully read, their difficult passages explicated in class, and their ideas commented upon by the professor and discussed by the students. For the University to impose limits upon such discussions and commentaries would, I am sure, have been unthinkable to Jefferson. He was not saying to professors and students, "Thus far shalt thou go, and no farther." He was in effect saying, "Let these great documents of our political heritage be your starting point. Let their ways of reasoning be the model and guide for your own thinking. Explore to the full the implications of what they have said. Prepare to test new ideas by the principles which you have thereby developed in your own minds. And on your own intellectual voyage into the future, God speed!"

The University resolution of Jefferson and Madison has another feature which should commend it to our attention. It states in clear and objective fashion precisely where one may discover the principles that are to be deemed legitimate. For lack of such a definition, a poisonous fog of uncertainty hangs over all measures dealing with loyalty at the present day. The private preconceptions and the secret prejudices of investigators take the place of known and recognized standards. One can become suspect for believing too firmly in the Declaration of Independence or the Fifth Amendment, one can be denounced for supporting particular decisions of the Supreme Court or particular acts of Congress, one can be condemned for expounding certain doctrines not merely of Jefferson but even of Alexander Hamilton or John Marshall. I have sometimes thought that one might escape condemnation by taking a firm and unequivocal stand in favor of the political and social philosophy of Rutherford B. Hayes, but even this might prove a frail reed to lean upon. Actually the only safe course today is to believe in the American system but not in any special part of it, to adore the Constitution as a whole but to avoid too close an acquaintance with or attachment for any of its specific provisions, to be loyal to the American tradition but not to be so misguided as to assert that any element in it is of any particular value or significance. If *this* is genuine loyalty, then in what does *dis*loyalty consist?

Jefferson and Madison, by contrast, knew the meaning of the maxim, *a government of laws and not of men.* They accepted the responsibility of pointing out where the sanctioned principles of government "are to be found legitimately developed." Should one be in doubt as to the kind of reasoning that is "generally approved" in the field of government, one is directed to the treatises of John Locke and

Algernon Sidney as models. Should one need a guide to "the distinctive principles" of the American system of government, one is directed to four fundamental documents which have stated them, each in a different way, in a different context, from a different point of view. Within these limits the honest inquirer might move with freedom and safety. The resolution was, in effect, a shield against false accusations and sly innuendoes. It protected a man against condemnation for statements which violated no fundamental principle but which merely presented conclusions that some powerful group happened to dislike. In the face of charges of disloyalty, the accused could appeal to a known standard, and could insist that the prosecutor prove that the doctrines expounded were in fact and in logic "incompatible with those on which the Constitutions . . . were genuinely based."

The University resolution of 1825 seems to me to embody a positive, affirmative approach to freedom. It was the approach which Jefferson characteristically employed, not merely in meeting educational problems, but in dealing with every aspect of the intellectual warfare that rages unceasingly between the ideals of liberty and the hostile, subversive ideas of tyranny and totalitarianism. As we fight the campaigns of our own day in this war against evil and darkness, we are in terrible need of the kind of affirmative program that Jefferson knew how to devise. Allow me to outline briefly what the strategy of such a positive defense of freedom might be.

Many citizens today are concerned about the possible weakening of loyalty through faulty teaching in our schools. There is a negative approach to this problem. It involves scrutinizing textbooks for possibly dubious passages. It involves questioning teachers to discover whether they harbor any unorthodox ideas. It involves closing off the discussion of controversial issues. Before long it engenders a universal dread of ideas themselves, lest certain ones prove perilous.

And in the end such a negative conception of education is bound to raise up a generation not of citizens but of innocent dupes, who may fall victim to almost any sort of demagoguery simply because their powers of discrimination, of criticism, and of independent thinking have never been exercised or developed.

The American Republic was not created by and cannot be preserved by men who are afraid of ideas. The great statesmen of our past were thoroughly acquainted with un-American ideas. They had to be if they were to meet them effectively. The one safeguard that Jefferson and Madison insisted upon was that the basic principles of our own system, the great documents of our own tradition, and the full history of our own development should be thoroughly understood, so that no man might surrender his heritage through ignorance of what it is and how it came into being. This, I think, is the positive safeguard we should really seek and insist upon today.

Let us look at our schools, not to purge them of ideas but to purge them of trivialities. Let us make sure that the history of our country, from its remotest origins to the present, is studied with the amplitude it deserves. Let us not be satisfied with a few pious generalizations about the Constitution, but make sure that in our schools the Constitutional Convention, the Constitution itself, and the crucial decisions of the Supreme Court throughout the years are fully analyzed and discussed. Let us not succumb to the fallacy that current events are the only events worth knowing, but insist that all the varied issues that have arisen in the three-hundred-and-fifty-year development of our national tradition be made understandable to young students. And let us make sure that our teachers are thoroughly equipped with the factual knowledge and the scholarly discipline to handle these questions intelligently and intelligibly. Rigorous examinations of every teacher's competence in these matters would provide a far more effective guarantee of the schools' contribution to good citizenship than any loyalty oath that can possibly be devised.

Many groups of citizens, finally, are concerned about libraries. It is proper that they should be. But they ought to search the shelves, not to unearth an occasional volume containing aberrant ideas, but to discover whether the basic books that embody the essence of the American tradition are universally available. Let patriotic groups inaugurate campaigns, not to remove certain books from our libraries, but to place certain books there. Two monumental works have appeared recently—the definitive set of the *Collected Works of Abraham Lincoln* and the magnificent edition of the *Papers of Thomas Jefferson,* which is steadily moving toward its ultimate goal of fifty-two volumes. These contain the materials that ought to be available to every American. How few, however, are the public libraries which can afford to purchase them! Instead of advertising the works that we deem subversive by seeking to ban them, why not concentrate our money and our time in an effort to place great sets like these in every public library in the land? And why not go on from there to fill the gaps that are to be found everywhere in the sections that ought to contain the writings of our statesmen, the standard histories of our country, and the great works of American biography and literature and political philosophy?[87] Let us emulate the Gideons, who do not ransack the hotel newsstand to get rid of literature they do not approve, but who quietly place a Bible in each hotel bedroom, trusting that in God's own time it will speak its message.

The negative way of defending freedom is monstrously futile. We can banish Robin Hood from our nurseries, we can delete one passage after another from our textbooks, we can burn such books of our enemies as we may find on the shelves of our libraries and information centers. But where can we stop? The Bible has subverted empires and establishments in the past. The Sermon on the Mount and the Acts of the Apostles contain passages from which conclusions deemed radical have been drawn time and time again. The Declaration of Independence is admittedly a revolutionary document. And the Constitution and its amendments enshrine ideas that have often frightened respectable but timid men. Are we to lock up these subversive texts and circulate carefully expurgated abridgments to the impressionable many? And if we do these things, what have we left? The tatters of a great tradition, waving wanly over a vast intellectual void.

This is not liberty and enlightenment. It is emptiness and gloom. Arrayed against us today are the powers of intellectual night. But who ever heard of pulling down the shades to shut out the darkness? Our salvation is to light the lamps and to keep them burning.

APPENDIX

Resolution on Textbooks, University of Virginia, 1825

The Complete Documentary Record

The following passages, transcribed directly from photographic reproductions of the original manuscripts, comprise all the known documents bearing upon the drafting and adoption of the resolution on textbooks which the Board of Visitors of the University of Virginia approved on March 4, 1825. Some parts are published for the first time.

I. THOMAS JEFFERSON TO JAMES MADISON, FEBRUARY 1, 1825

. . . In most public Seminaries a Text-book is prescribed to the several schools as the Norma docendi in them, and this is frequently done by the Trustees. I should not propose this generally in our Univ[ersi]ty because I believe none of us are so much at the heights of science in the several branches, as to undertake this, and therefore that it will be best left to the Professors, until occasion of interference shall be given. but there is one branch in which I think we are the best judges, and the branch itself is of that interesting character to our state and the US. as to make it a duty in us, to lay down the principles which are to be taught. it is that of gov[ern]m[en]t. even while mr Gilmer was considered as our choice, I received from many persons expressions of great uneasiness lest the doctrines of that school should have an improper bias. he was believed by some and strongly believed to be too much infected with the principles of the Richmond lawyers, who are rank Federalists as formerly denominated, & now Consolidationists. I do not believe this myself. I never heard an unsound opinion on gov[ern]m[en]t uttered by him. but now that he is withdrawn, and the successor uncertain, and a possibility has arisen that a Richmond lawyer, or some one of that school may be proposed, I think it a duty to guard against danger by a previous prescription of the texts to be adopted. I inclose you a resol[utio]n which I think of proposing at our next meeting, for your consid[eratio]n, with a prayer that you will correct it freely, and make it what you think it ought to be. . . .

Jefferson Papers, Library of Congress, folio 40836 (microfilm in University of Illinois Library). This is Jefferson's retained copy.

The enclosure, containing Jefferson's original draft of the resolution, is missing from this copy and also from both extant copies of the letter to Cabell (No. II below). Dr. Julian P. Boyd, editor of the *Papers of Thomas Jefferson,* informs me (letter of Nov. 30, 1953) that no copy of this original draft has yet been located in the course of the extensive research which the editorial staff has done in the preparation of this edition.

II. THOMAS JEFFERSON TO JOSEPH C. CABELL, FEBRUARY 3, 1825

. . . In most public seminaries Text-books are prescribed to each of the several schools as the norma docendi in that school; and this is generally done by authority of the Trustees. I should not propose this generally in our University, because, I believe, none of us are so much at the heights of science in the several branches as to undertake this; and therefore that it will be better left to the Professors until occasion of interference shall be given. but there is one branch in which we are the best judges, in which heresies may be taught, of so interesting a character to our own state and to the US. as to make it a duty in us to lay down the principles which shall be taught. it is that of Government. mr Gilmer being withdrawn, we know not who his Successor may be. he may be a Richm[on]d lawyer, or one of that school of quondam federalism, now Consolidation. it is our duty to guard against the dissemination of such principles among our youth, and the diffusion of that poison, by a previous prescription of the texts to be followed in their discourses. I therefore inclose you a resolution which I think of proposing at our next meeting; strictly confiding it to your own knolege alone and to that of mr Loyall, to whom you may communicate it, as I am sure it harmonizes with his principles. I wish it kept to ourselves, because I have always found that the less such things are spoken of beforehand, the less obstruction is contrived to be thrown in their way. I have communicated it to mr Madison. . . .

Jefferson Papers (originally from Cabell Papers), University of Virginia Library (photostat in University of Illinois Library). Jefferson's retained copy is in Jefferson Papers, Library of Congress, folio 40837 (microfilm in University of Illinois Library). So far as wording is concerned, the retained copy differs from the one sent only in the following phrases: "principles which are to be taught" instead of "which shall be"; "against such principles being disseminated among" instead of "against the dissemination of such principles among"; and "it will harmonize" instead of "it harmonizes." The enclosed resolution is missing in both copies.

III. JAMES MADISON TO THOMAS JEFFERSON, FEBRUARY 8, 1825

. . . I have looked with attention over your intended proposal of a text book for the Law School. It is certainly very material that the true doctrines of liberty, as exemplified in our Political System, should be inculcated on those who are to sustain and may adminster it. It is, at the same time, not easy to find standard books that will be both guides & guards for the purpose. Sydney & Locke are admirably calculated to impress on young minds the right of nations to establish their own Governments, and to inspire a love of free ones; but afford no aid in guarding our Republican Charters against constructive violations. The Declaration of Independence, tho' rich in fundamental principles, and saying every thing that could be said in the same number of words, falls nearly under a like observation. The 'Federalist' may fairly enough be regarded as the most authentic exposition of the text of the federal Constitution, as understood by the Body which prepared & the authorities which accepted it. Yet it did not foresee all the misconstructions which have occurred; nor prevent some that it did foresee. And what equally deserves remark, neither of the great rival parties have acquiesced in all its comments. It may nevertheless be admissible as a School book, if any will be that goes so much into detail. It has been actually admitted into two Universities, if not more, those of Harvard & Rh[ode] Island; but probably at the choice of the Professors, without an injunction from the superior authority. With respect to the Virginia Document of 1799, there may be more room for hesitation. Tho' corresponding with the predominant sense of the nation; being of local origin & having reference to a state of parties not yet extinct, an absolute prescription of it, might excite prejudices against the University as under party Banners, and induce the more bigoted to withold [*sic*] from it their sons, even when destined for other than the studies of the Law School. It may be added that the Document is not, on every point, satisfactory to all who belong to the same party. Are we sure that to our brethren of the Board it is so? In framing a political creed, a like difficulty occurs as in the case of religion tho the public right be very different in the two cases. If the articles be in very general terms, they do not answer the purpose: if in very particular terms, they divide & exclude where meant to unite & fortify. The best that can be done in our case seems to be, to avoid the two extremes, by referring to selected Standards without requiring an unqualified conformity to them, which indeed might not in every instance be possible. The selection would give them authority with the Students, and might controul or counteract deviations of the Professor. I have, for your consideration, sketched a modification of the operative passage in your draught, with a view to relax the absoluteness of its injunction, and added to your list of Documents, the

Inaugural Speech and the Farewell Address of President Washington. They may help down what might be less readily swallowed, and contain nothing which is not good; unless it be the laudatory reference in the Address, to the Treaty of 1795 with G[reat] B[ritain] which ought not to weigh against the sound sentiments characterizing it.

After all, the most effectual safeguard against heretical intrusions into the School of politics, will be an able & orthodox Professor, whose course of instruction will be an example to his successors, and may carry with it a sanction from the visitors.

Affectionately yours
James Madison

Sketch

And on the distinctive principles of the Government of our own State, and of that of the U. States, the best guides are to be found in 1. The Declaration of Independence, as the fundamental Act of Union of these States. 2. The book known by the title of the 'Federalist', being an authority to which appeal is habitually made by all & rarely declined or denied by any, as evidence of the general opinion of those who framed & those who accepted the Constitution of the U. States, on questions as to its genuine meaning. 3. The Resolutions of the General Assembly of Virg[ini]a in 1799, on the subject of the Alien & Sedition laws, which appeared to accord with the predominant sense of the people of the U.S. 4 The Inaugural Speech and Farewell Address of President Washington, as conveying political lessons of peculiar value; and that in the branch of the School of law which is to treat on the subject of Gov[ernmen]t these shall be used as the text & documents of the School.

Madison Papers, Library of Congress (photostat in University of Illinois Library).

IV. JOSEPH C. CABELL TO THOMAS JEFFERSON, FEBRUARY 11, 1825

Your favor of 3d inst. has been duly received, and your requests attended to. Both the letter and the enclosed resolutions have been shewn to Mr. Loyall, and to him alone. He will unite in supporting the resolution relative to the text books on government. . . .

Jefferson Papers (deposited by Philip B. Campbell), University of Virginia Library (photostat in University of Illinois Library).

V. THOMAS JEFFERSON TO JAMES MADISON, FEBRUARY 12, 1825

I concur with entire satisf[actio]n in your am[en]dm[en]t of my resol[utio]n, and am peculiarly pleased with your insertion of Gen[era]l Wash[ington]'s addresses, which had not occurred to me or I should have referred to them also. . . .

Jefferson Papers, Library of Congress, folio 40843 (microfilm in University of Illinois Library); Jefferson's retained copy.

VI. MINUTES OF THE BOARD OF VISITORS OF THE UNIVERSITY OF VIRGINIA, MARCH 4, 1825

At a special meeting of the Board of Visitors of the University, called by George Loyall, Chapman Johnson and Joseph C. Cabell while attending the late session of the legislature, and held at the University Mar. 4. 1825.

Present Thomas Jefferson Rector, James Madison, George Loyall, John H. Cocke, and Joseph C. Cabell. . . .

A Resolution was moved and agreed to in the following words.

Whereas it is the duty of this board to the government under which it lives, and especially to that of which this University is the immediate creation, to pay especial attention to the principles of government which shall be inculcated therein, and to provide that none shall be inculcated which are incompatible with those on which the Constitutions of this state, and of the US. were genuinely based, in the common opinion: and for this purpose it may be necessary to point out specifically where these principles are to be found legitimately developed:

Resolved that it is the opinion of this board that as to the general principles of liberty and the rights of man in nature and in society, the doctrines of Locke, in his 'Essay concerning the true original extent and end of civil government,' and of Sidney in his 'Discourses on government,' may be considered as those generally approved by our fellow-citizens of this, and of the US. and that on the distinctive principles of the government of our own state, and of that of the US. the best guides are to be found in 1. the Declaration of Independence, as the fundamental act of union of these states. 2. the book known by the title of 'The Federalist,' being an authority to which appeal is habitually made by all, and rarely declined or denied by any as evidence of the general opinion of those who framed, and of those who accepted the Constitution of the US. on questions as to it's genuine meaning. 3. the Resolutions of the General assembly of Virginia in 1799. on the subject of the Alien and Sedition laws, which appeared to accord with the predominant sense of the people of the US. 4. the Valedictory address of President Washington, as conveying political lessons of peculiar value. and that in the branch of the school of Law, which is to treat on the subject of Civil polity, these shall be used as the text and documents of the school.

University of Virginia, Minutes of the Board of Visitors, manuscript volume in Alderman Library, University of Virginia, pp. 78–79 (microfilm in University of Illinois Library). This entry is in the handwriting of Jefferson and is signed by him.

In a bundle of loose papers, preserved with the volume of minutes just quoted, is a copy of the resolution in Jefferson's hand, but unsigned and undated. The bundle was labeled by Jefferson "Minutes & Documents of the Session of Oct 1825." These loose papers comprise (*a*) notes made by Jefferson at the meetings and used by him in writing up the final minutes, and (*b*) documents presented to the board and later transcribed into the minutes. The draft in question was presumably the copy of the resolution which Jefferson took to the session of March 4, 1825. It is a fair copy, with no emendations or interlineations, therefore it must have been written after Jefferson had heard from Madison and had incorporated the latter's suggestions. Verbally the text is identical with that in the minutes, with only trifling variations in punctuation, capitalization, and abbreviation.

VII. JAMES MADISON TO W. A. DUER, SEPTEMBER —, 1833

I have rec[eive]d your letter of the 28th ult., inclosing the outlines of your work on the Constitutional Jurisprudence of the U.S. . . .

As an attention to the design of the work, is invited from me as "the Head of the University of Virginia" as well as an individual, it is proper for me to observe, that I am but the presiding member of a Board of Visitors; that the superintendence of the Institution is in the Faculty of Professors; with a chairman annually appointed by the Visitors; and that the choice of text & class books is left to the Professors respectively. The only exception is in the School of Law, in which the subject of Government is included; and on that the Board of Visitors have prescribed as text authorities: "the Federalist, the Resolutions of Virg[ini]a in 1798, with the comment on them in '99; and Washington's Farewell Address." The use therefore that will be made of any analogous publications, will depend on the discretion of the Professor himself. His personal opinions, I believe, favor very strict rules of expounding the Constitution of the U.S. . . .

Madison Papers, Library of Congress (photostat in University of Illinois Library).

"THE GREAT INVENTION OF THE WORLD":

MR. LINCOLN AND THE BOOKS HE READ

BY DAVID C. MEARNS

"This is emphatically the age of reading."—Joseph Story: *Science and Letters in Our Day*, 1826.

His Reading Habits

When the Honorable Abraham Lincoln, of Illinois, addressed a great Republican "concourse," in Kalamazoo, in the summer of 1856, he told his audience: "We stand at once the wonder and admiration of the world, and we must enquire what it is that has given us so much prosperity, and we shall understand that to give up that one thing, would be to give up all future prosperity. This cause is that every man can make himself." [1]

Four years later, this self-made man, recently nominated for the presidency of the United States, wrote of himself: "The agregate of all his schooling did not amount to one year. He was never in a college or Academy as a student;

and never inside of a college or academy building till since he had a law-license. What he has had in the way of education, he has picked up. . . . He regrets his want of education and does what he can to supply the want." [2]

By placing these statements in juxtaposition, it is easy to understand why his biographers have attached such extraordinary importance to Mr. Lincoln's reading. With less discrimination, objectivity, judgment, reason, skepticism than they have applied to any other aspect of his career, those biographers have borrowed recklessly from one another, and have cheerfully compiled a catalogue of impressive dimensions. But had Mr. Lincoln read, digested, absorbed all of the books imputed to him, he could not have been, as he was, the most gregarious of public men.

Beginning in the summer of 1860, with the interviews of William Dean Howells's stand-in, James Quay Howard, and intensifying in 1865, with the more searching interrogatories of William H. Herndon, there were residents, or former residents, of Hardin County, Kentucky; Spencer County, Indiana; and Coles and Sangamon counties, Illinois, who delighted to testify to Mr. Lincoln's early passion for reading. These gaffers were frequently specific, supplying the titles of works which had shaped Mr. Lincoln's mind; occasionally going so far as to cite actual imprints and editions. A few proudly produced the very copies which the prodigy had borrowed from them.

The memories of this "cloud of witnesses" were, in some instances, almost suspiciously unanimous, as though in leisure moments they had coached one another. There were cases, however, where they differed radically on particulars; and not infrequently their recollections were at such variance as to counsel disbelief and disdainful rejection. They were not always incapable of invention.

The evidence has only recently become generally available. Mr. Howard's findings were selected and used by Mr.

Howells and himself in producing their campaign biographies of the prairie paragon. Thereafter they passed to Robert Todd Lincoln who placed them at the disposal of John George Nicolay and John Hay while preparing *Abraham Lincoln: A History*. They did not become accessible to the public until midsummer 1947.

The information so assiduously gathered by William Henry Herndon was transcribed at least in part for Ward Hill Lamon, who turned it over to his ghost writer Chauncey Forward Black, who exploited it in an extended essay at denigration and bad taste, *The Life of Abraham Lincoln,* published in 1872. Seventeen years later, with help from a collaborator, Jesse W. Weik, *Herndon's Lincoln: The True Story of a Great Life* was published. In it, the materials on Lincoln's reading were made to subserve the dubious image conjured by the last law partner. Next to be permitted to see them was Albert J. Beveridge whose death closed a meticulous biography when his *Abraham Lincoln* had reached the year 1858. For a time they were in the possession of the late Emanuel Hertz who, in 1938, published a selection under the title *The Hidden Lincoln,* which, because of sometimes garbled renderings, did not release his hero from the hands of the special pleaders. The Herndon records were acquired by the government in 1941. They prove Herndon to have been at once a magnificent collector and a confused, perhaps a devious, interpreter.

Even now, when the original sources are open to everyone for study, the Lincoln mystery persists. When, for example, did Lincoln learn to read? In Kentucky, Lincoln had gone to school to Caleb Hazel. A neighbor, remembering the schoolteacher, wrote of him that he "could perhaps teach spelling, reading & indifferent writing & perhaps could cypher to the rule of three—but had no other qualifications of a teacher except large size & bodily strength to thrash any boy or youth that came to his school, and as Caleb lived in a Hazlenut Switch County no doubt but that young Abraham received his due allowances."[3]

THE MYSTERY OF HIS LEARNING TO READ

Mr. Lincoln's ebullient, omniscient, incredible cousin Dennis Hanks, on the other hand, wrote with sublime confidence: "About Abs early education and his sisters education let me say this. Their mother first learned them a b c's."[4] To accomplish this, Nancy Hanks Lincoln must have been divinely inspired for she "was absolutely illiterate."[5] But Hanks was explicit: "She learned them this," he insisted, "out of Websters old spelling book: it belonged to me & cost in those days 75c, it being bound with calf skin—or such like covering." Then, in the same letter, he injected this startling intelligence: "I taught Abe his first lesson in spelling—reading & writing." And he concluded this bio-bibliographical discourse by declaring: "Lincoln's mother learned him to read the Bible—study it & the stories in it and all that was moving & affectional in it, repeating it to Abe & his sister when very young. Lincoln was often and much moved by the stories. This Bible was bought in Philadelphia about 1801—by my Father & Mother & was mine when Abe was taught to read in it."[6]

A SPENCER COUNTY IDYL

Dennis's claim to distinction was not too much of a strain on gullibility to gain family acceptance. His son-in-law, Colonel Augustus H. Chapman, wrote with assurance:

> While living in Ind. his cousin D. F. Hanks learned him [i.e., Lincoln] to spell, Read & write. he afterwards went to school in Ind. about 5 months during one fall and winter & learned very fast making rapid progress in his studies. Often he studied long hours during his [leisure] hours, he procured a copy of Pike's arithmetic & mastered its entire contents with but little help from others. he also borrowed all the Books he could in the

neighborhood he . . . obtained a coppy of Barclay's Dictionary [1799] which aided him much in his studies. This Dictionary is still in the hands of his Step Mother in Charleston Ills as is also the old Family Bible [1818] of Thos Lincoln A Lincolns Father. he also wrote much at home writing rude verses of his own composition in his coppy books also working mathematical problems in his coppy Books.[7]

That the enlightenment imparted by Dennis Hanks may have been supplemented by the exertions of Mr. Lincoln's Hoosier schoolmasters is suggested by a fellow-pupil who recalled:

In the fall of 1818 the mother of Abraham and wife of Thomas Lincoln was taken sick with a desease called the Milk sickness or puken a desease commin at that time in the western country[.] her sickness was short but fatal as she deseas this life Oct 1818 leving Abraham and the rest of the family to morne the loss of a kind mother[.] Thomas Lincoln remaind on his little farm doing the best he could with his two children for a yeare or two[.] he then went to ky and married a second wife who was a widow Johnson, about this time there was a scool house built two miles south of Thomas Lincoln farm that was the first school house that was built in this part of the state[.] the house was built of round logs just high enough for a man to stand erect under the ruff, the floore was split logs or what we called punchens[.] the chimney was maid of poles and clay[.] the window was constructed by bye [*sic*] chopping out a part of tow [*sic*] logs and plasing peases of split bords at proper distance and then we would take our old coppy books and grease them and paste them over the windows[.] this give us lite[.] in this shool room Abraham Lincoln and my self entered school[.] the scool was taught bye a man named Andy Crofford [Crawford.] After that Abraham went to man by the name of Hayel Dausey [Azel W. Dorsey] also another bye the name of Swany [James Swaney.] these were all of the scool teachers that Abraham Lincoln was taught buy in this state[.] he was always at school early and atentive to his studies[.] he always was at the head of cllass[.] progressed rapedly in all of his studies[.] he lost no time at home[.] when he was not at work he was learning his books[.] he persued his studies on the Sabeth day[.] he also packed books when at work to read when he rested from laber[.] his habit of life[:] he was kind and clever to all[.] indeed he appeared to cultivate it as a prinsipal always being wel stored [with] witty sayings giving no offence to any one[.] he also rit while very young essays on bein cind to animals and crawling insects[.] he was always temperet in all of his habits[.] he was truthf[ul] and onest and industrious always working with his one hands when not at scool or studying at home . . . i am sorry that my naritive is so short but it is the best i can do for you so you must excuse me.[8]

But the evidence that, whatever his instruction or whoever his instructor, Mr. Lincoln first learned to read with any degree of satisfaction in the years when he resided in Indiana comes from Mr. Lincoln himself. When he stopped off at Trenton on his way to Washington and his first inauguration, he told the New Jersey Senate:

May I be pardoned if, upon this occasion, I mention that away back in my childhood, the earliest days of my being able to read, I got hold of a small book, such a one as few of the younger members have ever seen, "Weem's Life of Washington." I remember all the accounts there given of the battle fields and struggles for the liberties of the country and none fixed themselves upon my imagination so deeply as the struggle here at Trenton, New Jersey. The crossing of the river; the contest with the Hessians; the great hardships endured at that time, all fixed themselves on my memory more than any single revolutionary event; and you all know, for you have all been boys, how these early impressions last longer than any others. I recollect thinking then, boy even though I was, that there must have been something more than common that these men struggled for.[9]

The provenance of Lincoln's copy of the peddling parson's most memorable work became a family tradition. Colonel Chapman recounted it in his best manner:

The only work he ever done on the Crawford Farm in Ind. was as follows. He borrowed of Josiah Crawford the Life of Washington. While this Book was in his Lincoln's possession it got damaged by being wet & on his returning it to Crawford he Crawford refused to receave it and insisted on Lincoln paying him for the same which Lincoln agreed to do as he had not the money to pay for the same he worked for Crawford a puling corn Blades at 25 cts a day & thiss paid for the Damaged Book.[10]

When he lived on Pigeon Creek, Mr. Lincoln's reading followed no carefully formulated plan. It could not, conditioned as it was by such publications as might be borrowed near at hand. There were no book stores in the wilderness, no public libraries, and the specimens of literature in the possession of neighbors, only slightly if any better favored than he, had been preserved as much for sentimental reasons as for a love of learning. Still, Mr. Lincoln appears to have read whatever he could find, but beyond a few textbooks, anthologies, and half-forgotten miscellanea, which biographers have grimly resurrected from a comfortable oblivion, it was his good fortune to become acquainted with such familiar standbys as Aesop's *Fables, Pilgrim's Progress, Robinson Crusoe,* and Watts' *Hymns.*[11]

His youngest stepsister, Matilda Johnston More, remembered Sunday mornings: "When father and mother would go to church," she wrote, "they walked about 1–½ miles. When they were gone—Abe would take down the bible, read a verse—give out a hymn—and we would sing." Mrs. More felt certain that they "were good singers."[12]

Before Lincoln left his father's house to strike out for himself, his father did what he could to indulge and promote Lincoln's interest in books. Wrote his stepmother: "As a usual thing Mr. [Thomas] Lincoln never made Abe quit reading to do anything if he could avoid it. He would do it himself first. Mr. Lincoln could read a little & could scarcely write his name: hence he wanted, as he himself felt the uses &

necessities of education, his boy Abraham to learn & he encouraged him to do it in all ways he could." [13]

THE DAFT YOUTH OF NEW SALEM

In the summer of 1831, Abraham Lincoln, now on his own, went to live in a small community, high above a river, called New Salem. He soon established himself in the respect and affection of his fellow-townsmen, but his propensity for study was so intense and so at variance with local custom as to endow him with a reputation for harmless eccentricity. One inhabitant reported an odd baby sitter. "When I first saw Abraham Lincoln," he wrote, "he was lying on a trundle bed rocking a cradle with his foot—was almost covered with papers and books." [14]

Another noted that "he read aloud very often; and frequently assumed a lounging position when reading. He read very thoroughly, and had a most wonderful memory. Would distinctly remember almost everything he read. Used to sit up late of nights reading & would recommence in the morning when he got up. He was not an unusually early riser." [15]

Still another watched him while "reading, walking the streets, [he would] occasionally become absorbed with his book, would stop & stand for a few moments, then walk on, or pass from one house in the town to an other, or from one crowd of men to an other apparently seeking amusement, with his book under his arm, when the company or amusement became dry or irksome he would open his book & commune with it for a time, then return it to its usual resting place and entertain his audience." [16]

The former pilot of the *Talisman,* J. Rowan Herndon, was an excellent observer but an infamous orthographer; wrote he of Lincoln:

> he set up Late & Rose early[.] When nothing else ocipided [occupied] his time he was Reading some work or paper . . . he

scearsly ever went to Bed Before 12 and was up By Day Light and often set up Later . . . he was some times seting some times stading [standing] and some times on his Back and very [often] would walk Down to the River Reading when he would Return the same way iff Commenced Reading anything very intrusting he Jenerly Put it through and he allways Remembered what he Red.[17]

In New Salem Mr. Lincoln had more leisure for reading than he had had before or would ever have again. J. Rowan Herndon put it very succinctly: "As to the Books & Papers he Read they were such as he could Borrow," adding, "he had the use of such as had." Indeed, "he had axcess [*sic*] to any Books that was in and around the town." [18]

Another warm friend, Abner Y. Ellis, took a seemingly different, if not conflicting and confusing, view: "As to his own Books [I never] Knew of his having [any] excep[t] Law Books. . . . I never Knew of [his] Borrowing any Books & I do not th[ink] He Card [cared] much for those he had of mine." [19] But a week before making this statement, the former Postmaster had described certain books which he had lent to Mr. Lincoln.[20]

Yet the finest tribute came from his sometime instructor, Mentor Graham: "In New Salem he devoted more time to reading the scripture, books on science and comments on law and to the acquisition of knowledge of men & things than any man I ever knew and it has been my task to teach in the primary school Forty five years and I must say that Abraham Lincoln was the most studious, diligent strait [*sic*] forward young man in the pursuit of knowledge of literature than any among the five thousand I have taught in the schools." [21]

MR. KIRKHAM'S GRAMMAR

It is said that in the New Salem years "he studied Natural Philosophy, Astronomy, Chemistry, &c." [22] But of all the branches of learning, he applied himself with greatest concentration to three. The first was grammar. "After he was twenty three, and had separated from his father," he wrote of himself, "he studied English grammar, imperfectly of course, but so as to speak and write as well as he now does." [23]

This made a lasting impression upon his friends. Billy Greene told James Quay Howard, in 1860, that "2 or 3 mos. after he landed, said he would study grammar–good practical grammarian in three weeks." [24] Five years later, Billy expanded the theme for Billy Herndon:

> Soon after he landed and commenced clerking he took a notion to study grammar & surveying. I told him I had a grammar & surveying books at home. This remember was in the summer & fall of 1830. He went down with me and got them and instantly commenced his studies. Mr. Lincoln studied the grammar & surveying privately in his store—worked it out by himself alone as I recollect it, though others may have explained special problems—rules and such like things which he could not easily master. Mr. Lincoln soon mastered his grammar & the general rules . . . of surveying. He mastered them rapidly—like reading—so quick and comprehensive was his mind.[25]

Mentor Graham had a different version; he informed Howard that "when L. was about 22 said he believed he must study Grammar–one could not be obtained in the neighborhood–walked for 8 miles and borrowed Kirkham's old Grammar." [26] Then, in the spring of 1865, Graham, like Greene, amplified the account for the benefit of Herndon:

> In the month of February A.D. 1833 Mr. Lincoln came and lived with me & continued with me about six months. It was here that he commenced the study of English Grammer [*sic*] with me. I was then teaching school. . . . Mr. Lincoln spoke to me one day and said "I had a notion of studying English grammar." I replied to him thus "If you expect to go before the public in any capacity I think it the best thing you can do." He said to me "If I had a grammar I would commence now." There was none in

the village & I said to him—"I know of a grammar at one Vances about 6 miles" which I thought he could get. He was then at breakfast—ate—got up and went on foot to Vances & got the Book. He soon came back & told me he had it. He then turned his immediate & almost undivided attention to English Grammar. The book was Kirkham's grammar—an old volume, which I suppose—have so heard—is in the Rutledge family to-day. During the spring—summer & fall he read law—studied and practiced surveying and the grammar & would recite to me in the evening. I have taught in my life four or six thousand people as school master and no one ever surpassed him in rapidly—quickly & well acquiring the rudiments and rules of English grammar.[27]

Aside from the dates, Graham's story contradicted Greene's in two other details: (1) the manner in which Lincoln obtained the text; (2) the manner of his instruction. The first, Greene did not contest; but on the second point he was obdurate, assuring Herndon:

I still persist in the assertion that Mr. Lincoln had no Teacher after he came to New Salem[;] that he was self Taught[.] it may be true that & I suppose it is true that Mentor Graham a verry [*sic*] kind & communicative man did give Mr. Lincoln many explanations & elucidations both in English Grammar & Surveying just as John T. Stuart did in the Law[.] I have seen Graham since I rec'd your letter[.] he still persisted that he taught him but when I questioned him wher [*sic*] when & what school house he had to admit that it was on the street behind the counter when at dinner &c. &c[.] Just as you continually teach Law to enquiring friends friend Graham has always been remarkable for his willingness to instruct the Youth of the community in which he lived & I agin [*sic*] repeat that he has many times *based* Mr. Lincoln for hours as he a hundred times has your humble servant.[28]

This was bad enough, but there was still another tutorial contestant, Lynn McNulty Greene, who had told Howard: "Every time I went to Salem he [Lincoln] took me out on the hill and got me to explain to him Kirkham." [29] Lynn Greene, like Bill Greene and Mentor Graham, went into circumstantial detail when he wrote to Herndon: "In the summer after he came home from the Black Hawk War he got possession of one Kirkham's Grammers [*sic*] & began studying it on the hill sides of old Salem. I spent several days giving him instruction in this manner. In fact all the instruction he ever had in Grammer [*sic*] he rec'd from me." [30]

But there was still another claimant, Dr. Jason Duncan, who reported to Herndon:

> I first went to reside in New Salem in August A.D. 1831 to practice my profession [medicine] procuring an office room in the public house of James Rutledge. I became acquainted with Abraham Lincoln . . . shortly after my arrival . . . the winter following Abraham requested me to aid him in the study of English Grammar which I consented to do to the extent of my limited ability. his application through the winter was assiduous and untiring, his intuitive faculty was surprising. he seemed to master the construction of the english language and apply the rules for the same in a most astonishing manner.[31]

It is always difficult to be dogmatic about Abraham Lincoln, but in this case, who is to be believed? One of the Greenes, Graham, or Duncan? Perhaps Mr. Lincoln was taught by all of them; perhaps he required a faculty. On the other hand, when William Dean Howells wrote a biography for the 1860 campaign, he accepted the Graham version of the long walk for a copy, and Lynn Greene's version of hillside instruction. The fact that Mr. Lincoln did not change the statement in the copy of Howells which he corrected for Samuel C. Parks may mean that Howells was right. It is impossible ever to be sure.

In an undated letter, Robert B. Rutledge confirmed the survival of Mr. Lincoln's "Kirkham." He wrote to Herndon: "Mr. Lincoln studied Kirkham's Grammar—the valuable copy which he delighted to peruse is now in my possession." [32]

That little book is now in the Library of Congress. It is entitled: *English Grammar in Familiar Lectures, Accompanied by a Compendium; Embracing a New Systematick Order of Parsing, a New System of Punctuation, Exercises in False Syntax, and a Key to the Exercises: Designed for the Use of Schools and Private Learners. . . . Sixth Edition, Enlarged and Much Improved.* It was imprinted at Cincinnati by N. & G. Guilford in 1828.

Its first owner appears to have been Miller Arrowsmith, who commenced his study of it, June 8, 1829. His name appears at several places in the book. An inscription on the title page announces that "Ann M. Rutledge is now learning Grammar." On the verso of the title page is yet another inscription: "Martha A. Berry is now lurning [*sic*] Gramer [*sic*]." There are the scrawled signatures of Daniel C. Burns, Sarah C. Rutledge, and Faney (?) C. Rutledge. But there are no marks to identify it with one Vance or with Abraham Lincoln. This is purely negative; there is no reason to disregard its distinguished provenance as asserted by Robert Rutledge.

A SANGAMON SURVEYOR

Mr. Lincoln next took up the subject of mathematics. William G. Greene described an interview which went like this: "Said to me Bill if that [i.e., grammar] is what they call a science I'll subdue another–Asked about authors on surveying told him Stuart's was good– borrowed it." [33] But Greene's inference that Mr. Lincoln was motivated primarily by mere intellectual curiosity is incorrect. Moreover, so far as can be ascertained, no Stuart ever wrote a textbook on surveying.

Mr. Lincoln himself was more explicit. He had failed as a storekeeper. The New Salem postmastership was no sinecure. He was obliged to earn a living. It was a relief, therefore, when "the Surveyor of Sangamon offered to depute to

A that portion of his work which was within his part of the county. He accepted, procured a compass and chain, studied Flint, and Gibson a little, and went at it. This procured bread, and kept soul and body together." [34]

Abel Flint's *System of Geometry and Trigonometry with a Treatise on Surveying* and Robert Gibson's *Theory and Practice of Surveying* were popular texts. Again Mentor Graham was expositor.

> After the canvas [*sic*] of 1832 [Graham recalled] Mr. Lincoln turned his attention exclusively to the law—surveying—History—Biography & general newspaper reading. . . . In . . . 1833 Mr. Lincoln came & lived with me . . . I taught him the rules of surveying. I do not think Mr. Lincoln was [knew] any thing of arithmetic—especially of geometry & trigonometry before he came to my house, and I think I may say he was my schollar & I was his teacher.[35]

BLACKSTONE AND HIS COMMENTARIES

Thereafter, according to his chronicler, Billy Greene: "Said he, if I thought the law was as easy as these [i.e., grammar and surveying], I would commence it–wanted to get hold of something that was knotty." [36]

On the other hand, there are those who maintain that Mr. Lincoln's interest in the law was aroused long before, in the Indiana days. Dennis Hanks, for example, wrote: "I had like to forgat how Did Abe get his Knowledge of Law this is the fact a Bout it I Bought the Statute[s] of Indiana and from that he Lerned [*sic*] the principles of Law and allso [*sic*] My self." [37]

Herndon himself published to the world a slightly different version: "The first law book Lincoln ever read was 'The Statutes of Indiana.' He obtained the volume from his friend David Turnham, who testifies that he fairly devoured the book in his eager efforts to abstract the store of knowledge that lay between the lids. No doubt, as Turnham insists, the study of the statutes at this early day led Abe to think of the law as his calling in maturer years." [38]

There is no reference to this book in Turnham's letters to Herndon, but it is stated that Turnham presented it to Herndon on September 1, 1865.[39] Herndon, in turn, deposited the copy in the Lincoln Memorial Collection of Chicago. It was in "a dilapidated form, wanting title-page and several leaves at end," but was accompanied by an autograph letter from Herndon guaranteeing "its authenticity." It was sold at auction in 1894,[40] where it was acquired by William Hoffman Winters of the New York Law Institute.[41]

It is difficult, if not impossible, for a layman to understand how a reading of "The Revised Laws of Indiana, Adopted and Enacted by the General Assembly of Indiana At Their Eighth Session" could impart to Mr. Lincoln "the principles of law" or could arouse ambition for a legal career. But because the prefatory matter contained the texts of the Declaration of Independence, the Constitution of the United States, and the great Ordinance of 1787, it is conceivable that from it Mr. Lincoln secured his introduction to American institutions.

Mr. Lincoln himself ascribed to Major John T. Stuart, his comrade in the Black Hawk War and future partner, credit for having encouraged him to study law. After the election of 1834 when he was elected to the Illinois Legislature, he . . .

> borrowed books of Stuart, took them home with him, and went at it in good earnest—He studied with nobody—He still mixed in the surveying to pay board and clothing bills—When the Legislature met, the law books were dropped, but were taken up again at the end of the session. He was re-elected in 1836. . . . In the autumn of 1836 he obtained a law license, and on April 15. 1837 removed to Springfield, and commenced the practice.[42]

The people of New Salem would never forget with what

resolution he had there pursued his study. William Butler, for one, recalled a conversation:

> Asked him what he would do if he had money—Said he would first pay his debts, and then would like to study law—but did not see how he could do it, as he had no books or influential friends—said that every body wished him well—but he never could ask a man for a favor—I saw that he was an honest and worthy young man, and took him into my family and for three years treated him the same as my son—I paid his debt of $400, which L was not aware of till almost a year afterwards—Got him books and clothes and encouraged him in study of law.[43]

Henry McHenry, for another, remembered how "he read law sometimes–always during good weather–in the open air: he sat on a goods box under a large white oak tree in Salem, barefooted as he came into the world: Lincoln would come out & stay with me a week or two at a time, reading law." [44]

Mr. Lincoln may be presumed to have begun his professional training by reading Blackstone's *Commentaries*. Lynn Greene insisted that "the first Law Book that Lincoln ever read was a copy of Blackstone belonging to Vincent A. Bogue who once packed pork at Beardstown & died soon after." [45]

Dr. Jason Duncan was similarly unequivocal: "The first law books which Lincoln owned were purchased by him at a sheriffs sale at Springfield consisting of a copy of Blackstone's Commentaries. After he purchased those books he determined to make the profession of law his pursuit." [46]

Henry McHenry's testimony substantiated the testimony of Dr. Duncan: "In 1833 [he was off at least a year], I think went to Springfield and bought at an auction a copy of Blackstone. When he began to study law he would go day after day for weeks and sit under an oak tree on hill near Salem, and read–moved round tree to keep in shade–was so absorbed that people said he was crazy." [47]

But Allan J. Conant, the artist, made it appear an accident, dredging up a thirty-three-year-old memory:

In the year 1860, about two months before the presidential election, I was requested by the Hon. William M. McPherson, of St. Louis, to go to Springfield and paint the portrait of the standard-bearer of the new Republican party . . . . Among the incidents of his earlier life which Mr. Lincoln related [was this:]

"One day a man who was migrating to the West drove up in front of my store with a wagon which contained his family and household plunder. He asked me if I would buy an old barrel, for which he had no room in his wagon, and which he said contained nothing of special value. I did not want it, but to oblige him I bought it, and paid him, I think, half a dollar for it. Without further examination, I put it away in the store and forgot all about it. Some time after, in overhauling things, I came upon the barrel, and emptying it upon the floor to see what it contained, I found at the bottom of the rubbish a complete edition of Blackstone's Commentaries. I began to read those famous works, and I had plenty of time; for during the long summer days, when the farmers were busy with their crops, my customers were few and far between. The more I read,"—this he said with unusual emphasis, "the more intensely interested I became. Never in my whole life was my mind so thoroughly absorbed. I read until I devoured them." [48]

Mr. Conant's story was picturesque; it has been delightedly appropriated by numerous biographers; but it is so opposed to chronology and fact as to be ridiculous. Where, then, did Mr. Lincoln get his first Blackstone? Perhaps he borrowed it from Major Stuart, but it seems more likely that he obtained it at the sheriff's sale. He did not modify the statement to that effect in Howells's *Life of Abraham Lincoln*.

To one correspondent, Mr. Lincoln wrote:

Yours . . . asking "the best mode of obtaining a thorough knowledge of the law" is received. The mode is very simple, though laborious and tedious. It is only to get the books, and read, and study them carefully. Begin with Blackstone's Commentaries, and after reading it carefully through, say twice, take up Chitty's Pleading, Greenleaf's Evidence, & Story's Equity &c. in succession. Work, work, work is the main thing.[49]

This advice, excellent no doubt, is hard to reconcile with Herndon's astonishing assertion: "I doubt if he [i.e., Lincoln] ever read a single elementary law book through in his life. In fact, I may truthfully say, I never knew him to read through a law book of any kind." [50]

But Mr. Lincoln had another view. To a student he once confided:

I am from home too much of my time, for a young man to read law with me advantageously. . . . I did not read with any one. Get the books, and read and study them till, you understand them in their principal features; and that is the main thing. It is of no consequence to be in a large town. I read in New-Salem, which never had three hundred people living in it. The *books*, and your *capacity* for understanding them, are just the same in all places.[51]

PUBLIC MAN OF SPRINGFIELD

"I am not an accomplished lawyer," [52] he once confessed, but there can be no doubt that he held his profession in high honor. He had resided in Springfield only a few months when, in the course of an address to the Young Men's Lyceum, he declaimed with unusual rhetorical abandon:

Let every American, every lover of liberty, every well wisher to his posterity, swear by the blood of the Revolution, never to violate in the least particular, the laws of the country; and never to tolerate their violation by others. As the patriots of seventy-six did to the support of the Declaration of Independence, so to the support of the Constitution and the Laws, let every American pledge his life, his property, and his sacred honor;—let every man remember that to violate the law, is to trample on the blood of his father, and to tear the character [charter?] of his own, and his children's liberty. Let reverence for the laws, be breathed by every American mother, to the lisping babe, that prattles on her lap—let it be taught in schools, in seminaries, and in colleges;—let it be written in Primmers, spelling books, and in Almanacs;—let it be preached from the pulpit, proclaimed in legislative halls, and enforced in courts of justice. And, in short, let it become the *political religion* of the nation; and let the old and the young, the rich and the poor, the grave and the gay, of all sexes and tongues, and colors and conditions, sacrifice unceasingly upon its altars.[53]

Abraham Lincoln was on his way. Henceforth his aspirations would be fixed upon preferment at the gift of the electorate. Grammar and law had prepared him for a future: these and a genius for relationships, the powers of which he perfectly understood. For to him, people and politics were (as perhaps they should be) one and inseparable. What, after all, were politics but the service of the people's cause? And yet, it may be well to keep in mind this concept when considering the reading habits of a surpassing statesman.

Back in New Salem the possession of books had not attracted him.[54] He would never become, in the general sense, a collector. "He had," wrote Herndon of the Springfield householder, "aside from his law books and the few gilded volumes that ornamented the centre table in his parlor at home, comparatively no library." And Herndon added: "He never seemed to care to own or collect books." [55] Actually those "few gilded volumes" meant so little to Mr. Lincoln that on the eve of his departure for his first inauguration, he gave "a large part of his literary library" to Herndon.[56] They were irretrievably dispersed when "The Private Library! of W. H. Herndon, Esq. (former law partner of Hon. Abraham Lincoln)" was sold at auction in Cincinnati, January 10 and 11, 1873.[57] These, for the most part, had been gifts; they bore no signs of having exerted any special significance upon their more distinguished proprietor.

No, Abraham Lincoln was never a bibliophile. For him, books were not objects of virtue to keep, treasure, and cherish. They existed only to be read. When read, they had discharged their purpose. A friend of his maturity, Joseph Gillespie, put it this way:

> Study with Mr. Lincoln was a business not a pleasure. He was extremely diligent when he had anything to do in preparing himself but when the task was done he betook himself to recreation. The information he gathered was in reference to special questions and not with a view of laying in a general store of knowledge expecting that he would have occasion to use it and yet his natural tastes and aptitudes led him to explore most of those departments of study which bore mainly on the practical affairs of life.[58]

Milton Hay, who had studied law in Lincoln's office, concurred in the verdict. "I do not think he was ever a general reader," wrote Hay. "He read such Books only as lay in his way, as he might have opportunity to read, or were in the direction of his tastes." [59] But he appears consistently to have reserved a part of his busy life for the solace, diversion, or enlightenment of reading. His first law partner, John T. Stuart, gave an account of his custom when away from home:

> Mr. Lincoln commenced carrying around with him on the Circuit—to the various Courts, books . . . as early as 1844 and continued to do so down as late as 1853 . . . In the evening Lincoln would strip off his coat and lay down on the bed—read—reflect and digest—after supper he would strip—go to bed—get a candle—draw up a chair or a table and read till late at night: he read hard books . . . . he read specially—dug out things . . . Lincoln was a schollar from 1835—rather a hard student to 1845 —He was an educated man in 1860—more than is generally known.[60]

DISCOVERIES AND INVENTIONS

In February, 1859, a few months after the close of the

Debates with Douglas, on the day before his fiftieth birthday, and exactly two years previous to the delivery of his farewell to Springfield, Mr. Lincoln gave his *Second Lecture on Discoveries and Inventions.* That remarkable document abounds with references to the subject of this discourse; it is appropriate, therefore, indeed it is necessary, to quote from it *in extenso*:

> Writing—the art of communicating thoughts to the mind, through the eye—is the great invention of the world. Great in astonishing range of analysis and combination which necessarily underlies the most crude and general conception of it—great, very great in enabling us to converse with the dead, the absent, and the unborn, at all distances of time and space; and great not only in its direct benefits, but greatest help, to all other inventions. Suppose the art, with all conception of it, were this day lost to the world, how long, think you, would it be, before even young America could get up the letter A. with any adequate notion of using it to advantage? The precise period at which writing was invented, is not known, but it certainly was as early as the time of Moses; from which we may safely infer that its inventors were very old fogies.

He had conducted a reading aptitude experiment upon himself; this he reported as follows:

> It may be of some passing interest to notice the wonderful powers of the *eye,* in conveying ideas to the mind from writing. Take the . . . example of the numbers from *one* to *one hundred,* written down, and you can run your eye over the list, and be assured that every number is in it, in about one half the time it would require to pronounce the words with the voice; and not only so, but you can, in the same short time, determine whether every word is spelled correctly, by which it is evident that every separate letter, amounting to eight hundred and sixty-four, has been recognized, and reported to the mind; within the incredibly short space of twenty seconds, or one third of a minute.

And he credited, though he did not name him, Gutenberg

with having been man's Intellectual Emancipator, writing:

> At length printing came. It gave ten thousand copies of any written matter, quite as cheaply as ten were given before; and consequently a thousand minds were brought into the field where there was but one before. That was a great *gain;* and history shows a *change* corresponding to it, in point of time. . . . The effects could not come all at once. It required time to bring them out; and they are still coming. The *capacity* to read, could not be multiplied as fast as the *means* of reading. Spelling-books just began to go into the hands of children; but the teachers were not very numerous, or very competent; so that it is safe to infer they did not advance so speedily as they do now-a-days. It is very probable—almost certain—that the great mass of men at that time, were utterly unconscious, that their *conditions,* or their *minds* were capable of improvement. They not only looked upon the educated few as superior beings; but they supposed themselves to be naturally incapable of rising to equality. To immancipate [*sic*] the mind from this false and under estimate of itself, is the great task which printing came into the world to perform. It is difficult for us, *now* and *here,* to conceive how strong this slavery of the mind was; and how long it did, of necessity, take, to break it's shackles.[61]

Those who seek a charter for the freedom to inquire, the freedom to inform, and the freedom to read will find no better statement than this.

He expressed it differently, a few months later, when he spoke before the Wisconsin State Agricultural Society, at Milwaukee: "A capacity, and taste, for reading," he there remarked, "gives access to whatever has already been discovered by others. It is the key, or one of the keys, to the already solved problems. And not only so. It gives a relish, and facility, for successfully pursuing the [yet] unsolved ones."[62]

WASHINGTON

In the White House, Mr. Lincoln's reading was governed

by events. A private secretary, John Hay, recorded, perhaps carelessly, that "he read very little. Scarcely ever looked into a newspaper—unless I called his attention to an article on some special subject. He frequently said 'I know more about this than any of them.' It is absurd to call him a modest man. No great man was ever modest. It was his intellectual arrogance and unconscious assumption of superiority that men like Chase and Sumner never could forgive." [63]

It was nonsense to assert that "he read very little." Actually, he was constantly reading: there were those dispatches from the captains in the field, memoranda from cabinet ministers and lesser officers, criticisms from friendly and hostile editors alike, petitions of every sort and kind, appeals for clemency, claims on patronage, the occasional words of encouragement. These could not be neglected. And there were the proceedings of a watchful, impatient, inquiring Congress which must be followed. There was public clamor to heed. There was private selfishness to answer. Once, at least, the burden became intolerable; to a lady he wrote:

> It is difficult for you to understand, what is, nevertheless true, that the bare reading of a letter of that length requires more than any one person's share of my time. And when read, what is it but an evidence that you intend to importune me for one thing, and another, and another, until, in self-defence, I must drop all and devote myself to find a place, even though I remove somebody else to do it, and thereby turn him & his friends upon me for indefinite future importunity, and hindrance from the legitimate duties for which I am supposed to be placed here? [64]

The mere writing of that protest was probably enough to vent Mr. Lincoln's wrath. It is unlikely that the letter was ever sent.

Yet, despite the pressures of his office and his wearing days, Mr. Lincoln found time for books. At the White House, at Soldiers' Home, returning by steamer from City

Point, Mr. Lincoln would sometimes entertain his company by reading aloud.

Mrs. Lincoln replenished the shelves of the Executive Mansion, Mr. Lincoln sharing the expense of her purchases with the federal appropriation for the purpose.[65] From the fact that so many works of Mr. Lincoln's favorite authors were represented by new editions, it is possible that he referred to them from time to time.

During the war years, more than 125 loans were made by the Library of Congress to the account of Abraham Lincoln, president of the United States. A few of these may have been used in the preparation of messages to the Senate and the House, a few more may have been withdrawn for the President's diversion, but from a cursory study of the titles, it seems clear that most of them were borrowed for members of the Lincoln family or for his secretariat.

At an early hour, one summer morning, a passerby saw the President standing behind the White House gate. Mr. Lincoln called to him: "Good-morning, good-morning! I am looking for a newsboy; when you get to the corner I wish you would start one up this way." [66] The carrier would bring him the story of a people, one of whom he was. Fragments of it no doubt were in his pocket when he sat there in the theater watching.

His Reading Tastes

Mr. Lincoln's choice of literature reflected a complicated, inhibited, extroverted, strangely variable nature. It had, to be sure, its constancies, but there were inconsistencies as well, and these derived from migrant moods. No contemporary whose evidence survives ever saw him at every period of his life or observed his every humor. But some drew erroneous impressions of his taste by creating a principle from an isolated instance. This was perilous, not only because the premise itself was sometimes utterly false, but because it was sometimes partially true.

Mr. Lincoln was forever growing; which is to say that he was forever outgrowing. In maturing, his interests changed; a few intensified, more were superseded. A catalogue of the books which, at one time or another, passed under his eye, however interesting as a bibliographical essay it may be, cannot explain Mr. Lincoln's becoming.

Certainly his taste was by no means as catholic as it has been represented to be. There were subjects to which he was indifferent and of which he was therefore ignorant. But there were others that captured his imagination and shaped his spirit. Because this was so it may be well to consider, albeit briefly and inadequately, his attitude toward some of the branches of literature.

HISTORY

Writing of Lincoln in New Salem, J. Rowan Herndon noted that "he Read all of histry [*sic*] that he could Get hold of," adding that the local merchants "all had a fare [*sic*] lot of history and he had full axcess [*sic*] to any and all and Made Good use of them." [67] But so loyal a friend of later years as John T. Stuart would insist that he "didn't know anything about history—had no faith in it nor biography." [68] This recalls Mr. Lincoln's remark that "history is not history unless it is the truth." [69] Perhaps he had been disenchanted by some romance masquerading as Clio. But another intimate, Joseph Gillespie, was probably correct when he wrote: "Mr. Lincoln never I think studied history except in connection with politics[.] with the exception of the history of the Netherlands and of the revolutions of 1640 & 1688 in England and of our revolutionary struggle he regarded it as of triffling [*sic*] value as teaching by example." [70]

This feeling may account for the fact that the copies of

Gibbon's *Decline and Fall* (New York, 1839) and Hallam's *View of the State of Europe During the Middle Ages* (New York, 1837), translated from the center table in Springfield to the Huntington Library, are both inscribed by Mr. Lincoln as gifts from Ninian W. Edwards, but contain no other signs of opening.

But Mr. Lincoln appears to have skimmed Marryat's *Diary in America* [71] and to have made an inaccurate transcript of the lines to the desirable and "bright mulatter," Sally Brown, for the benefit of the Springfield Scott Club.[72]

Certainly, when preparing formal addresses and messages, Mr. Lincoln turned to American historical sources for precedent, allusion, or quotation.

This is illustrated by an episode recounted by Charles Sumner in an obituary of George Livermore:

> At a critical moment, before the government had determined to enlist colored soldiers, he [Mr. Livermore] prepared and printed at his own expense a most instructive elucidation of this question, founded on our revolutionary history, which he entitled "An Historical Research Respecting the Opinions of the Founders of the Republic on Negroes as Slaves, as Citizens, and as Soldiers." This was read to the Massachusetts Historical Society 14 August 1862, two months before the first proclamation of emancipation, and nine months before the famous 54th Regiment of Massachusetts, commanded by Colonel Shaw, sailed from Boston. Among the agencies which swayed the public mind at that time this publication cannot be forgotten, and it is within my own knowledge that it interested President Lincoln much. The President expressed a desire to consult it, while he was preparing the final proclamation of emancipation, and, as his own copy was mislaid, he requested me to send him mine, which I did.[73]

Another example of his resort to history is contained in Herndon's account of Mr. Lincoln's preparation of his Cooper Institute Address:

> He searched through the dusty volumes of congressional proceedings in the State library, and dug deeply into political history. He was painstaking and thorough in the study of his subject. . . . It is said by one of his biographers, that those afterwards engaged in getting out the speech as a campaign document were three weeks in verifying the statements and finding the historical records referred to and consulted by him. This is probably over-stated as to time, but unquestionably the work of verification and reference was in any event a very labored and extended one.[74]

In connection with politics, history had its uses.

BIOGRAPHY

Mr. Lincoln grew cynical about biography, but it is reported that, in New Salem, he studied the lives of Washington, Jefferson, Clay, and Webster,[75] and that he borrowed from James Short a copy of Amos Blanchard's anonymously published *American Military Biography,* "which he read a great deal." [76] At some time he became acquainted with William Wirt's *Sketches of the Life and Character of Patrick Henry,* and as late as the fall of 1862, could quote a passage from it almost exactly.[77]

But his perusal of campaign biographies probably brought about disenchantment. These, including his own, he found amusing but politically dangerous because they could easily be turned to ridicule. What fun he must have had with the *Life and Services of General Pierce, Respectfully Dedicated to Gen'l Lewis Cass,* published at Concord by the Gazette Press in 1852. In a speech before his Whig friends he jeered: "Forthwith also appears a biographical sketch of him, in which he is represented, at the age of seventeen, to have spelled 'but' for his father, who was unable to spell it for himself." [78]

And among the notes in the copy of William Dean Howells's *Life of Abraham Lincoln* which Mr. Lincoln corrected for Samuel C. Parks are such comments as "wholly wrong" and "no harm, if true; but, in fact, not true."

Herndon told how in 1856 he had purchased a life of Edmund Burke. He had forgotten the author's name, and it is now too late to repair his memory. But for modern students it can be supplied: James Prior.[79] Let Herndon take it from there:

> One morning Lincoln came into the office, and, seeing the book in my hands, enquired what I was reading. I told him, at the same time observing that it was an excellent work and handing the book over to him. Taking it in his hand he threw himself down on the office sofa and hastily ran over its pages, reading a little here and there. At last he closed and threw it on the table with the exclamation, "No, I've read enough of it. It's like all the others. Biographies as generally written are not only misleading, but false. The author of this life of Burke makes a wonderful hero out of his subject. He magnifies his perfections—and suppresses his imperfections. . . . In most instances they [i.e., the biographers] commemorate a lie, and cheat posterity out of the truth.

Put Mr. Lincoln down as a man suspicious of biography.

RELIGION AND PHILOSOPHY

Among the first books which Thomas Lincoln purchased for his son was said to have been a Bible.[80] He read a Bible in New Salem. He read a Bible in Springfield. In Washington, according to Noah Brooks: "The Bible was a very familiar study with the President, whole chapters of Isaiah, the New Testament, and the Psalms being fixed in his memory, and he would sometimes correct a misquotation of Scripture, giving generally the chapter and verse where it could be found. He liked the Old Testament best, and dwelt on the simple beauty of the historical books." [81]

No doubt he knew it thoroughly. He often quoted from it.[82] Upon receiving a Bible from a group of Loyal Colored

People of Baltimore, he described it as "the best gift God has given to man. All the good the Saviour gave to the world was communicated through this book. But for it we could not know right from wrong. All things most desirable for man's welfare, here and hereafter, are to be found portrayed in it." [83]

It is doubtful if he ever forgot the hymns of Isaac Watts which he and his stepsister had sung so long ago.[84]

Much has been made by some writers of his having read Volney and Tom Paine.[85] But *The Ruins* and *The Age of Reason* were extremely popular and generally distributed. Perhaps Mr. Lincoln was merely keeping up.

According to "a usually reliable source," he "was a lover of many philosophical books and particularly liked Butler's Analogy of Religion, Stuart Mill on Liberty, and he always hoped to get at President Edwards on the Will." [86]

Jesse W. Fell gave him the sixteenth edition of William E. Channing's *Works* (Boston, 1859), but there is no sign of usage in any of the three volumes.[87] There may be reservations concerning his rumored passion for philosophy.

MATHEMATICS

Mr. Lincoln had a mathematical bent. The first pages in *The Collected Works* (an edition chronologically arranged) are given over to the surviving leaves of his neatly kept sum book, prepared when in his teens. (His study of surveying has already been reported in this paper.)

In his third-person autobiography, Mr. Lincoln announced with obvious satisfaction, and as evidence of adult education that "he studied and nearly mastered the Six-books of Euclid, since he was a member of Congress." [88]

Was he mistaken in his timing? Milton Hay wrote: "At the time I was in his office '39 and '40, he had in the office a copy of Euclid, and in his leisure moments he would demonstrate problems therefrom. This he could do on a first effort without much difficulty." [89]

THE CLASSICS

Did Abraham Lincoln read, in translation, the classic literature of Greece and Rome? He once made it very clear that he attached no particular importance to "the exact shade of Julius Caesar's hair." [90]

But in 1920, the late Talcott Williams, A.B. and A.M. Amherst; honorary A.M. University of Pennsylvania; L.H.D. Amherst, Western Reserve University, and Brown University; LL.D. University of Pennsylvania, Hobart College, Western Reserve University, Franklin and Marshall College; and Litt.D. University of Rochester, broke some startling news in the pages of *The American Review of Reviews.* This was the story:

> He [i.e., Lincoln] read Homer in the winter of 1859-60 in Bohn's translation. Julius Heath Royce, my father-in-law, a man of business at Albion, N.Y., spent the winter at Bloomington, Ill., where he had property. He was at the same hotel as Lincoln, who was in attendance at court. Day by day Mr. Royce, a man who never met any man without leaving a friend behind, saw Lincoln reach across the table for the hotel castor, set it before his place and lose himself in a volume, bound in dark cloth. Breakfast, dinner and supper brought the same absorption. He asked Lincoln what he was reading. He looked up with alert attention. "I am reading Homer, the Iliad and Odyssey. You ought to read him. He has a grip and he knows how to tell a story." Better criticism has not been made by one no nearer than a translation. Across the years since I heard this story and noted it, it has recurred to me and I record it now as the type of reading which changed his style and gave him the Attic simplicity and Hellenic elevation of his closing and deathless utterances.[91]

Mr. Lincoln was in Bloomington on the evening of April 10, 1860, and may have remained there through the twelfth, attending the McLean County Circuit Court, but if he ever read Homer it is amazing that it never shone through.

He quoted Plato as having "a pleasing hope—a fond desire—a longing after" immortality,[92] and he quoted the lines of Terrence: "Attempt the end and never stand to doubt; /Nothing so hard but search will find it out"; [93] but he may have come upon them in some anthology, gift annual, or other secondary source.

Soon after the Republican convention of 1860, a Chicago journalist, John Locke Scripps, hurriedly compounded a biography of that party's candidate for the presidency. It included a relation of the youthful Lincoln's servitude on Josiah Crawford's farm in payment for the damaged memoir of Washington (Scripps changed the authorship from Weems to Ramsey) and continued:

> Not long after this incident, he [Lincoln] was fortunate enough to get possession of a copy of Plutarch's Lives. What fields of thought its perusal opened up to the stripling, what hopes were excited in his youthful breast, what worthy models of probity, of justice, of honor, and devotion to great principles he resolved to pattern after, can be readily imagined by those who are familiar with his subsequent career, and who have themselves lingered over the same charmed page.[94]

But Scripps felt at least some dubiety concerning his clairvoyant powers. On July 17, he wrote to Mr. Lincoln: "I believe the biography contains nothing that I was not fully authorized to put into it. In speaking of the books you read in early life, I took the liberty of adding Plutarch's Lives. I take it for granted that you have read that book. If you have not, then you must read it at once to make my statement good." [95]

Five years later, Scripps told Herndon:

> When the pamphlet was printed, I sent a few copies to Mr. Lincoln, and in an accompanying note, I said to him I was in

doubt only as to one statement I had made—and that was as to whether or not he had read Plutarch's Lives. I had trusted somewhat to my memory on the subject of his early reading, and while I was not certain he had enumerated this book among those he had read in his boyhood, yet as I had grown up in about such a settlement as he had in Indiana, and as I had read Plutarch in my boyhood, I presumed he had had access to it also. If I was mistaken in this supposition, I said to him, it was my wish that he should at once get a copy, and read it, *that I might be able to testify as to the perfect accuracy of the entire sketch.* Mr. Lincoln did not reply to my note, but I heard of his frequent humorous allusions to it.[96]

Poor Scripps! He might have been comforted to know that from April 7 until July 29, 1862, someone at the White House had on loan from the Library of Congress a copy of the Clough edition of Plutarch.[97] It was charged to Abraham Lincoln's account!

FICTION

One day in 1864, Mr. Lincoln was conversing with Ira Harris and Francis Carpenter when he remarked: "It may seem somewhat strange to say, but I have never read a novel in my life! . . . I once commenced 'Ivanhoe,' but never finished it." [98]

No doubt, by some definition of his own, Mr. Lincoln's statement was the truth, but to the Lincoln student it raises as many questions as it answers. For according to Herndon's *Lincoln*: "He had a . . . pronounced fondness for fictitious literature, and read with evident relish Mrs. Lee Hentz's novels, which were very popular in that day, and which were kindly loaned to him by his friend A. Y. Ellis. The latter was a prosperous and shrewd young merchant who had come up [to New Salem] from Springfield and taken quite a fancy to Lincoln." [99]

Had Mr. Lincoln been mistaken, or had Abner Ellis been a shaky witness? In January, 1866, Ellis wrote to Herndon:

he read this Novel George Balcomb [i.e., *George Balcombe* by Nathaniel Beverley Tucker] in New Salem. . . . Oh yes I once loned [*sic*] him some Play Book[s] to read[.] I have them yet[.] They was as follows

The Wept of the Wishton Wish [*The Wept of Wish-ton-wish;* a tale by James Fenimore Cooper].

[The] Lady or [i.e., of] Lyons [by Bulwer-Lytton].

[The] Illustrious Strange[r] [an operatic farce by James Kenney].

[The] Hypocrite [by Isaac Bickerstaffe].

Poor Pillicoddy [by John Madison Morton].[100]

A few weeks later, Ellis wrote to Herndon again: "He borrowed those plays of me while I was P. M. . . . the novel he must have read before he came to Springfield." [101]

In a third letter, evidently in response to Herndon's entreaty for precise details, Ellis deposed:

Those fancy storys [*sic*] he bord [borrowed] of me was I think while I was in the P.O. except one and that was I think in 1837. I remember it was the Mob Cap by Mrs. [Caroline Lee (Whitney)] Hentz and at another time I loned [*sic*] him one of Bullyers [Bulwer's] Novels Now a Play Calld [*sic*] The Lady of Lyons.

Those that I loned [*sic*] him when I was P.M. was Plays, he returned them and I think he had read some of them. He said he had seen the Illustrious Stranger Played in Washington.[102]

It was something of a feat for Mr. Ellis to lend Mr. Lincoln a copy of *The Mob Cap and Other Tales* in 1837, because it appears to have been first published at Philadelphia by Peterson, in 1850.

But in a fourth letter, Ellis betrayed his uneasiness: "As to what he read I Cant [*sic*] say for Certain. I think He Said he had read George Balcom [*sic*] (a novel) . . . He and I was taking [talking] about some passages in it." [103]

This would seem to be enough to acquit Honest Abraham of brashness and to dismiss the Ellis-Herndon fiction that he read fiction. John T. Stuart, with more confidence, insisted that "he had nothing Rhetorical in his nature—no belles letters." [104]

It would, of course, be foolish to argue that because he quoted, "God tempers the wind to the shorn lamb," [105] he must therefore have read Sterne's *Sentimental Journey*. But when, in the course of a speech, he said, "Being philosophical and literary men, they have read, and remembered, how the institution of chivalry was ridiculed out of existence by its fictitious votary Don Quixote," [106] is there not a suggestion that he had read Cervantes' master work?

If Lincoln never read a novel, what becomes of those repeated assertions that he read *Robinson Crusoe*?

If Lincoln never read a novel, did he sometimes read short stories? According to Howells: "The bent of his mind . . . is mathematical and metaphysical, and he is therefore pleased with the absolute and logical method of Poe's tales and sketches, in which the problem of mystery is given, and wrought out into every-day facts by processes of cunning analysis. It is said that he suffers no year to pass without the perusal of this author." [107]

To his other qualifications for the presidency, Mr. Lincoln may have added an affection for whodunits, and thereby to have set an example for his successors.

POETRY

Those long-lived and erstwhile companions who, in later years, trafficked in remembering Lincoln were agreed that he had an inexhaustible, if sometimes curious, appreciation of poetry. Best of all they remembered his admiration for Burns and Shakespeare, and frequently mated those outward incompatibles in their commentaries.

Billy Greene, for example, said, in 1860, that Mr. Lincoln, while in New Salem "was always reading Burns and Shakespeare. Knew all of Burns by heart." [108]

Five years later Billy repeated himself, but with an odd variation: "Shakespear—Burns & Byron were his favorite books. He nearly knew Shakespear by heart." [109]

In some way it must have bothered Billy. He couldn't get it out of his mind and he couldn't tell which was which. Within a few months he wrote again: "Mr. Lincoln read Shakespear, Byron & Burns all extensively while he lived at Salem. I should say that Burns was his favorite." [110]

Abner Ellis indicated that Mr. Lincoln was a persistent fellow, writing that "he used to read Shakespear & Burns in Springfield." [111]

Howells conjoined the Scot and the Englishman when he wrote his book: "Before his [i.e., Lincoln's] election to Congress a copy of Burns was his inseparable companion on the circuit; and this he perused so constantly, that it is said he has now by heart every line of his favorite poet. He is also a diligent student of Shakespeare, 'to know whom is a liberal education.' " [112]

Milton Hay thought that Mr. Lincoln "could very nearly quote all of Burns' Poems from memory." He had frequently heard him recite "the whole of 'Tam O'Shanter,' 'Holy Willie's Prayer' and large portions of the 'Cotter's Saturday Night'." According to Hay, Mr. Lincoln "had acquired the Scotch accent and could render Burns perfectly." [113]

There can be no doubting Mr. Lincoln's enthusiasm. He thought it "wonderful" that a friend of his had actually "seen and known a sister of Robert Burns." He wanted to be told "something about her." [114]

Burns humbled Mr. Lincoln who once protested: "I can not frame a toast to Burns. I can say nothing worthy of his generous heart and transcending genius. Thinking of what he said, I cannot say anything which seems worth saying." [115]

As to the first gentleman of Stratford, Mr. Lincoln once confessed: "Some of Shakespeare's plays I have never read; while others I have gone over perhaps as frequently as any unprofessional reader. Among the latter are Lear, Richard Third, Henry Eighth, Hamlet, and especially Macbeth. I think nothing equals Macbeth." [116]

It is odd that he was so profoundly moved by the assassin's tragedy. A young Frenchman, on board the *River Queen*, recorded how . . .

On Sunday, April 9th [1865], we were proceeding up the Potomac. That whole day the conversation turned on literary subjects. Mr. Lincoln read aloud to us for several hours. Most of the passages he selected were from Shakespeare, especially *Macbeth*. The lines after the murder of Duncan, when the new king falls a prey to moral torment, were dramatically dwelt on. Now and then he paused to expatiate on how exact a picture Shakespeare here gives of a murderer's mind when, the dark deed achieved, its perpetrator already envies his victim's calm sleep. He read the scene over twice.[117]

Mr. Lincoln's copy of Shakespeare (New York, James Conner, 1835) is now in the Folger Library at Washington.[118]

His closest friend, Josh Speed, wrote of Lincoln, "I do not think he had ever read much of Byron previous to my acquaintance with him," but "he was a great admirer of some of Byron's poetry—Childe Harold, the Bride of Abydos, Mazeppa & some of his fugitive pieces." [119]

He seems to have enjoyed about equally the two elegies: Gray's "In a Country Churchyard," [120] and Goldsmith's "On the Death of a Mad Dog." [121]

James Grant Wilson gave him a copy of his friend Fitz-Greene Halleck's poems. Mr. Lincoln was very pleased, and with his thanks informed the donor that "many a month has passed since I have met with anything more admirable than his beautiful lines on Burns." [122] It was said that he "loved Halleck's Poem." [123]

On Thursday, May 22, 1862, Mr. Lincoln embarked on a journey to visit the army at Fredericksburg. With him were the Secretary of War, Mr. Stanton, and Admiral John A.

Dahlgren. The trip was so secret that "Mrs. Lincoln alone knew about it." In the evening, on shipboard, Mr. Lincoln read aloud from the "new edition" of Halleck (New York, 1861) the stirring verses of "Marco Bozzaris." [124] That copy is now in the collection of the late Foreman M. Lebold, of Chicago.

The poetry of the Breakfast Table's Autocrat held charms for Mr. Lincoln. His old companion on the circuit, Henry Clay Whitney, once wrote to Herndon:

> Dr. Oliver Wendell Holmes of Boston is quite anxious that it should be incorporated in your life of Lincoln the high estimation he had for his poem "The Last Leaf":—of course you know that it was a great favorite of Mr. Lincolns [*sic*]—& Gov [*sic*] Andrew of Massachusetts says that in the darkest days of our history while he was in consultation with Lincoln that the latter repeated to him the Entire poem: excuse me for mentioning the matter but it is so proper that it should find a place in your life of Lincoln—& Dr. Holmes is so justly anxious that it should do so that I could not avoid bringing it to your attention.[125]

To which Herndon gushed reply:

> I thank you for yours of the 30th ult., and would like to insert Mr. Holmes' Poem in my biography; but I have not his consent to do it. I have heard Lincoln recite it—praise it—Laud it, and swear by it: it took Mr L in all moods, and fastened itself on him as never poem on man. This I know. If you please you may drop Mr. Holmes—a gentleman whose character I love and whose genius I admire, a line stating my wishes. I am not acquainted with the gentleman and am somewhat sensitive about obtruding on "big men." Our courts are now in full blast. Ask Mr. Holmes to address me a note.[126]

In talking with Francis Carpenter, on the evening of March 25, 1864, Mr. Lincoln is reported to have said, "There are some quaint, queer verses, written, I think, by Oliver Wendell Holmes, entitled, 'The Last Leaf,' one of which is to me inexpressibly touching." At which point he recited from memory:

The mossy marbles rest
On the lips that he has pressed
  In their bloom
And the names he loved to hear
Have been carved for many a year
  On the tomb.

As he finished, he said emphatically: "For pure pathos, in my judgment, there is nothing finer than those six lines in the English language." [127] Other poems of Holmes which Lincoln liked were "September Gale," "The Chambered Nautilus," and "The Ballad of an Oysterman." [128]

Once when Agassiz called at the White House, and the conversation turned to philology and words in different languages with roots identical with English words, the President offered by way of illustration an anecdote which he had found in Thomas Hood's "Up the Rhine." Mr. Lincoln was pleased with some of Hood's lighter verse; particularly with "Faithless Sally Brown" (not to be confused with Marryat's mulatto of the same name) and "Miss Kilmansegg and Her Precious Leg." Indeed, "latterly Mr. Lincoln's reading was with the humorous writers." [129]

He came upon Longfellow's "Birds of Killingworth" in a newspaper, clipped, and carried it about in his vest pocket, reading it from time to time, until he had committed it to memory. He was also fond of the "Psalm of Life." [130]

As to James Russell Lowell, it is said that Mr. Lincoln could repeat word for word the whole of "John P. Robinson, he," and found sublime "originality and daring impudence" in Lowell's stanza:

"Ef you take a sword and dror it,
  An' stick a feller creetur thru,
Gov'ment hain't to answer for it,
  God'll send the bill to you." [131]

Poe's "The Raven" first appeared in the *Evening Mirror* for January, 1845. More than a year later, Mr. Lincoln wrote that he had "never seen" it,[132] but eventually he caught up with it, "read and loved" it, "repeated it over and over," and "carried Poe around on the circuit." It was thought that "he read Poe because it was gloomy." [133]

At least five times in his own writings, Mr. Lincoln quoted Alexander Pope. His copy of the *Poetical Works* (Philadelphia, 1839), a gift from Ninian W. Edwards, was one of the "gilded volumes" which Mr. Lincoln turned over to Herndon when he went to Washington. Herndon gave it, in 1867, to James T. Fields, of Boston. It is now in Harvard's Houghton Library.[134]

While riding with the President and Mrs. Lincoln, Nathaniel Parker Willis was once agreeably surprised when the President, "of his own accord," mentioned Willis's "Parrhasius" and proceeded to quote several lines from it.[135]

William Knox's mortuary offering, "Oh, Why Should the Spirit of Mortal Be Proud?" had special meaning for Abraham Lincoln. Whether it was philosophical or aesthetic, sentimental or superstitious, may never be known; perhaps he never analyzed his veneration for it, but it ran deep in his being. "I would give all I am worth, and go in debt," he wrote, "to be able to write so fine a piece as I think that is." Where and under what circumstances had he discovered it? "I met it," he recorded in April, 1846, "in a straggling form in a newspaper last summer, and I remember to have seen it once before, about fifteen years ago, and this is all I know about it." [136]

But if he had found it "in a straggling form" in 1845, and had seen it but once about fifteen years before, how had he been able to memorize it, quote it, transcribe it, and give it notoriety? Its authorship was frequently ascribed to him.[137]

On a March night, in 1864, in the office of the solicitor of the treasury, Mr. Lincoln is reported to have said to Francis

Carpenter: "The poem was first shown to me by a young man named 'Jason Duncan,' many years ago." [138] It is surprising that Carpenter could have been so exact. "I did not even keep a record of incidents," he wrote, "but simply a pocket diary of my work from day to day. By referring to this however various incidents would return to me." [139]

Following the publication of Carpenter's memoirs, he and Herndon had in the closing days of 1866 and extending to March 28, 1867, an extensive correspondence, but Carpenter did not refer to the poem. Herndon sent him a copy of his recent lecture on Ann Rutledge (which shocked him a little) and gave him Mr. Lincoln's copy of Byron.

The lecture, delivered in the Sangamon County Court House, November 16, 1866, mentioned the poem:

> Dr. Jason Duncan, of New Salem about September A.D. 1833, had shown and placed in Mr. Lincoln's hands the poem called in short, now, "Immortality," or properly, "Oh, Why Should the Spirit of Mortal be Proud?" Remember, Miss Rutledge died on the 25th of August, A.D. 1835 . . . He [i.e., Lincoln] went to New Salem about the last of September, A.D. 1835. He now once more picked up, took up, and read, and re-read the poem called "Immortality" . . . He saw new beauties in it. He seized it, and it seized him—a mutual seizure and arrest. He learned, learned it by heart, committed it to memory, and repeated it over and over to his friends.[140]

And when Herndon's *Lincoln* was published, it contained this passage:

> It was shortly after this [Ann Rutledge's death] that Dr. Jason Duncan placed in Lincoln's hands a poem called "Immortality." The piece starts out with the line, "Oh! why should the spirit of Mortal be proud." Lincoln's love for this poem has certainly made it immortal. He committed these lines to memory, and any reference to or mention of Miss Rutledge would suggest them, as if "to celebrate a grief which lay with continual heaviness on his heart." [141]

Had a romantic attachment existed between Mr. Lincoln and Miss Rutledge, Herndon's explanation of Mr. Lincoln's mournful, nostalgic, honorific, and pious reverence for the poem would be perfectly explained. But modern critics (the "higher critics") dismiss the love affair as a myth, Herndon's learned editor declaring, "Of reliable evidence touching upon the romance itself, there is not the slightest particle." [142] Moreover, Jason Duncan's long and undated memorandum in the Herndon-Weik Manuscripts (f. 3866) alludes to Lincoln's "great partialities for Miss Ann Rutledge," but nowhere refers to Knox's poem. With passion and sorrow removed, the basis for Mr. Lincoln's eccentric devotion to this unexceptional dirge remains a mystery.

How well, after all, did Mr. Lincoln know the poem? His memory was said to be prodigious, even photographic, but in ending his eulogy on Zachary Taylor with extracts from it, there were variants from the standard text; [143] when he dictated it for Francis Carpenter, he omitted two verses; [144] and when he transcribed it for Lois Newhall, he reversed two lines and inverted two verses.[145]

It is said that while in office he disclaimed authorship: "I should not care much for the reputation of having written that, but would be glad if I could compose music as fit to convey the sentiment as the words do now." [146]

NEWSPAPERS

Abraham Lincoln, postmaster of New Salem, "spent the time mostly of Knights in Reading history and Day tim [*sic*] News Papers for he generly [*sic*] Read for the By standers when the male [*sic*] Come which was weekly." [147] Colonel Chapman, speaking with an in-law's authority, announced that "he Lincoln first became a reader of newspapers after he came to Ills. The first newspaper which he took and read regularly was the National Intelligencer published at Washington City. of this paper he was a warm admirer." [148] That would be encouraging to believe, for it would establish an early interest in national affairs. But William Dean Howells, without demur from Mr. Lincoln, stated flatly: "The first publication for which he ever subscribed, was the *Louisville Journal,* which he paid for when he could secure the intellectual luxury only at the expense of physical comfort."[149] Howells probably relied upon the assurance of George Close: "His favorite paper was the 'Louisville Journal,' which he for many years studied—and paid for when he had not money enough to dress decently."[150]

Later on, Lincoln and Herndon, eagerly absorbed by the rising anger of the North and South, took the *Chicago Tribune,* the *New York Tribune,* the *Anti-Slavery Standard,* the *Emancipator,* and the *National Era,* which echoed their sectional views; and kept up with separatist tempers through the pages of the *Charleston Mercury* and the *Richmond Enquirer.*[151]

Lincoln's reading habits caused his partner great distress; wrote Herndon:

> When he reached the office, about nine o'clock in the morning, the first thing he did was to pick up a newspaper, spread himself out on an old sofa, one leg on a chair, and read aloud, much to my discomfort. Singularly enough Lincoln never read any other way but aloud. This habit used to annoy me almost beyond the point of endurance. I once asked him why he did so. This was his explanation: "When I read aloud two senses catch the idea: first I see what I read; second, I hear it, and therefore I can remember it better."[152]

During the war, three Washington papers were daily placed on his desk: the *Chronicle,* the *Republican,* and the *Star.* Mr. Lincoln would glance at the headlines, but rarely read further. The important news from the front reached him long before it went to press. John Hay and John Nicolay kept him up-to-date on significant editorial pronouncements.[153]

LINCOLN'S READING AND POLITICS

As an "old pol," Abraham Lincoln had a clear sense of the importance of looking at the record. As a member of the House, he sent a complete file of the *Congressional Globe* to Springfield, with instructions to "be careful to preserve all the numbers." [154] He had an interest in government documents of all kinds. He once asked a correspondent to procure the *Journal* and *Debates* of the New York Constitutional Convention of 1821.[155] On another occasion he looked all over Springfield, in behalf of a friend, for a copy of the President's Messages, and reported that the only one to be found was in the State Library, "and, of course, can not be had." [156]

He wrote a blurb for Andrew W. Young's *The American Statesman* (New York, 1857), which he had cursorily examined: "I think it may be safely said that the volume is invaluable to those desirous of accurate and full references to the political history of our country." [157]

In his forensic efforts he frequently appealed to the patristic writings of the Republic's founders.[158] He relied heavily on Jonathan Elliot's *Debates on the Adoption of the Federal Constitution* when preparing his Cooper Institute Address,[159] and when about to draft his first inaugural, he borrowed "Henry Clay's great speech delivered in 1850; Andrew Jackson's proclamation against Nullification, and a copy of the Constitution; 'later calling' for Webster's reply to Hayne, a speech which he read when he lived in New Salem, and which he always regarded as the grandest specimen of American oratory." [160]

It is likely that he kept up with the controversial literature of the day; he would almost have had to; it is very probable that he read Helper's *Impending Crisis.*[161] In the spring of 1858, a few months before the Debates with Douglas, Mr. Lincoln read a copy of Theodore Parker's *The Effect of*

Slavery on the American People: A Sermon Preached at the Music Hall, Boston, on Sunday, July 4, 1858 . . . Revised by the Author (Boston, William L. Kent & Company, 1858). On the fourteenth and final page, Mr. Lincoln found a sentence which he marked with a pencil: "Slavery is in flagrant violation of the institutions of America—Direct Government—over all of the people, by all the people, for all the people." [162] It would recur to Mr. Lincoln when, five years later, he considered what he would say at the dedication of that cemetery.

But when his habits and his tastes are carefully studied, when the witnesses and their testimony have been examined, when fact has been isolated from fancy or faulty recollection, and when wishfulness gives way to reality, there can be no reason to set aside Herndon's solemn judgment: "The truth about this whole matter is that Mr. Lincoln read *less* and thought *more* than any man in his sphere in America. . . . I repeat, that he read less and thought more than any man of his standing in America, if not in the world." [163]

FRANKLIN DELANO ROOSEVELT AND BOOKS

BY JONATHAN DANIELS

A man who reads books is a sufficiently suspicious character. A president with a library now may be as suspect as Mr. Jefferson's books were when he undertook to sell them to the Library of Congress, or rather to a Congress which some thought needed a library. That is today one klieg-lit point of view. There is another. We Americans are not only a suspicious people sometimes; we are a romantic one always—perhaps never more so than now. I doubt that we are ever more romantic about anything than books and education, unless it be the presidency. And today it seems to me there are clear evidences (of which these lectures may be a part) of a feeling that they should be put together—by public demand if not constitutional process. In the expanding institution of the presidency the president is already, of course, the decorative chief of state, administrative head of the government, commander-in-chief of the army and navy, leader of foreign affairs, and guide of public opinion. There is also a feeling, perhaps more prevalent among Platonists than plowmen, that somehow the president ought to be also the leader and embodiment of a kind of national great books program. Perhaps Mr. Jefferson set the pattern. And certainly, regardless of the realism and scholarship with which David Mearns discusses Lincoln's reading, I suspect we will all still keep in our heads the image of Lincoln reading the masterpieces with his forelock practically in the fireplace. All other great presidents must conform.

The simple fact is that already by public demand the institution of the presidency includes its occupant's function as chief bookman of the Republic. It is not a new function, but it was clearly staffed and crystallized best under Franklin Roosevelt. He was the man to whom the book dealers officially presented the best books published in America year by year. It was his job, of course, to issue a statement hailing the four hundredth anniversary of the first English Bible. It was his business to dedicate the shrine of Mark Twain in Hannibal, Missouri, and in effect speak the national critique of his work. Roosevelt did not invent the fiction, but it was the public expectation that when he used a literary allusion he should say that he "ran across" it in Bryce's *American Commonwealth* or "I went back and found a very nice thing" in Livy. He was expected to suggest what sort of books should be contributed in a collection for servicemen.

The institution is there. Fortunately, I think, in Roosevelt's case the man was, too. To that query about books for soldiers, he said, "Anything but algebras." For a president, I think, that approximates the wisdom of Mark Twain when he was asked to suggest a book list. You remember that he said, "Any book list is a good one which does not include *The Vicar of Wakefield*." I am not sure that Roosevelt would have agreed, though apparently he had some difficulties with the *Vicar* while at Groton. I do know that in a lesser sense, like Mark Twain, he escaped from that solemnity about books which is the first necessity of a book-loving man. Books were a part of his vernacular, not merely his erudition. He got the name for his mountain wartime hide-out, Shangri-La, from James Hilton's novel. And he gave the secret service headquarters there a name after Sherlock Holmes's address on Baker Street. In his speeches he sometimes said he "ran across" the resounding quotations from the great witnesses that he required, but, in this lecture series particularly, it pleases me to remember that he sent my fellow speaker Mr. Mearns searching through Edward Lear, Eugene Field, W. S. Gilbert, Alexander Woollcott and others to find the source of "the Cherable Isles" which he had whimsically added to a list of the places he told newspapermen he might visit on a cruise in 1940. It turned out, apparently to Roosevelt's own surprise, that he himself was the originator and discoverer and christener of those mythical islands. I think, however, that Mr. Mearns, whose great scholarship has never been limited to Lincoln, at least matched the presidential whimsey when he reported:

> To hunt for an island named Cherable,
> Is a job that is almost unbearable;
> Pray accept my apologies,
> But nonsense anthologies
> Are giving us hemorrhages cerebral.

I could call Mr. Mearns forward as witness though no witness seems necessary, to support the declaration that anybody who expects to find in any discussion of Roosevelt and books a simple, solemn presidential design will be disappointed. There have been more learned men in the presidency. I doubt, however (looking doubtfully only at Jefferson), if there was ever a more bookish man than Roosevelt in the White House. He liked books as objects. Sometimes he was impressed by the sheer bulk of collections, including particularly his own. He declined to be awed even by great libraries, however, and when a librarian of the Library of Congress resigned in wartime to take a post in the State Department, he commiserated with him on his "jump from one mausoleum into the other." Obviously, books and bookishness with such a man were not mere presidential manifestations.

Roosevelt's book story was the story of his life. He was born not merely with a silver spoon in his mouth but with all the standard, solid, respectable sets of books serried about his boyhood. Personally, I found it pleasant to learn that though he moved through a boyhood full of reading opportunities and educational advantages, he could not at fifteen spell Thomas de Quincey's name and brought a laborious attitude toward the Sir Roger de Coverly Papers. Clearly, however, he was a bookman long before he was out of Harvard. He liked to remember that he was librarian of the Hasty Pudding Club. Also, at that time he was librarian of the Fly Club. I'm not sure whether he mixed them up later or was then librarian of both. It was as such a club librarian, however, that he said he acquired his relationship to books as collector. He acquired it, he said later, from "old man Chase of N. J. Bartlett & Company" in Boston, who not only sold him books but gave him the advice, "Never destroy anything." Apparently he never did. As an undergraduate, also under "old man Chase's" guidance, he became a collector of rare editions. Bartlett's according to Roosevelt's son and the editor of his letters, "began as a drugstore, afterwards becoming a sort of student's supply store." Certainly its book counters were not restricted to paperbacks. Young Franklin strained his finances buying "a very nice old edition of Smollett" and early editions, too, of Junius' *Letters* and Dryden's *Virgil.* Also, he bought there as a student "the best possible set of Morte d'Arthur & very hard to get." Such references are undoubtedly going to be valuable items to some historian working on the lofty institution of the presidential bookman. I confess that the business of a young man seeking books for their age rather than for their content seemed a little more depressing than stimulating to me in the Roosevelt story, until I found that in FDR's undergraduate years he sent his precious editions home to his mother to keep safely but was very grateful to her for sending to him his well-loved though certainly not rare copy of Ernest Thompson Seton's *Rolph in the Woods.*

The bookman did not, it seems fortunate to me, overcome the healthy and definitely not highbrow reader. Even Dickens' *Christmas Carol* was not so much a part of Roosevelt's reading as of his Christmas ceremonials. The book about which Roosevelt seemed most enthusiastic as a boy was one by Anthony Hope. And there was Kipling. Some day someone may write a nice little essay on Roosevelt's lasting interest in that poet and panegyrist of empire. He pops up often in the letters. Roosevelt was shocked, as he should have been, when such a well-brought-up New England girl as Katherine Hepburn came as a movie actress to the White House and admitted she had never heard of *The Brushwood Boy.* There was something special and a little mysterious about Roosevelt's feeling for Kipling. While he was president he asked his ambassador to the Court of St. James's if he happened to know the then aging English author.

"If you do, I should like to get a note to him asking him a question I have long wanted to know the answer to."

Why, as president of the United States, he felt the need for an escort to his note seems a little strange. I have not been able to discover either the Roosevelt question or the Kipling answer. Both would be interesting. Two years later Kipling was dead, and Roosevelt wrote in a memorandum that he had been suggested for membership in the French Academy in Kipling's place. That, too, seems to me a little mysterious, perhaps even romantic. The story in his memorandum was that there was only some question of his right to accept it under the Constitution. There can be no question that he would have loved to occupy such a place among the literary "immortals."

It is his interest in Kipling which makes me question the influence on him attributed to some ponderous and less lively works. The yeast of imperialism was already stirring in the world and around Roosevelt when he was given as a Christmas present, when he was fifteen and could not spell De Quincey's name or remember the title of his book, a copy of Admiral Alfred Thayer Mahan's *The Influence of Sea Power Upon History*. Undoubtedly Mahan's book met and served the rising feeling about America's role as a world power, which was always ready among Roosevelts. The book did not originate it. Like many other writers who are presumed to have influenced presidents or just people, Mahan, I suspect, voiced well what was already widely felt. It would be interesting in connection with all presidents to compile a list of the so-called influential books which sold well not because they were influential but because already-influenced people were at hand. That might be tried on *Uncle Tom's Cabin*, maybe *Das Kapital*, and some others.

However, as a white water and high breeze man Roosevelt did clarify his feelings around Mahan's ideas, as did his Uncle Theodore and a good many others. Roosevelt was at one time influenced, too, as a young official, by that strange, hunchbacked soldier of fortune, prophet or phony, Homer Lea. His book *The Day of the Saxon,* which presented the yellow peril as what seemed later a sort of prediction of Pearl Harbor, stirred Roosevelt as a young man. Interestingly, however, at a point between the book and the bombs, FDR was one of those most convinced that there was no danger of an Asiatic attack. Certainly in the 1920's Roosevelt was enthused if not influenced by Claude Bowers' books, *Jefferson and Hamilton, The Party Battles of the Jackson Period, The Tragic Era*. Clearly, however, as energetic Democratic politician as well as enthusiastic book reviewer, he himself was less influenced by them than he hoped they would influence other people to be Democrats. Like the abolitionists who bought *Uncle Tom's Cabin,* Democrats were waiting for Bowers—and contrary to a general impression there are Democrats who not only can buy books but read them. Bowers' *Tragic Era,* about Reconstruction in the South, Roosevelt thought should be specifically useful in bringing back southern Democrats who had been frightened off to Hoover by Al Smith and the bogy of the Pope. Maybe it was. There were some other little details, however, like the price of cotton and the distance of prosperity from the corner.

There is a widespread feeling that the meaning of Roosevelt's reading in preparation for the presidency must be divided into two periods, the voracious reading in the leisure of his boyhood and the enforced reading in the long convalescence from infantile paralysis. In the recently published *Secret Diary of Harold Ickes,* the old curmudgeon recited testimony that in the pre-paralysis days Roosevelt was just a playboy who, as a vice-presidential candidate, would not even write his speeches—preferring to play cards. Then during his long illness he "began to read deeply." ("Deeply" is always a favorite word about presidential reading.) Undoubtedly Roosevelt did read then. He did have an enforced leisure, though not so empty a time as is often supposed. I think, however, that in regard to books and other things as well, the shrewdest historians will find basis for real suspicions about the sentimental legend that, in Roosevelt's case, infantile paralysis played a part in American politics like that of St. Paul's seizure on the road to Damascus in the story of Christendom. Roosevelt was already on the road he followed. Most of his basic reading was already done.

Roosevelt the bookman was certainly already formed. In large part he already had perhaps the finest collection of

American naval books and pamphlets in private hands anywhere. Already, I think, beyond the reading of his boyhood and his occasional use of great books as tools, his attitude to books had become that of the book collector, never the bookworm. He was fascinated by an attractive volume, the binding, the design, the print and the paper—particularly the rarity. Also, he had a positive addiction for labeling and cataloguing books. Much has been said about his relaxation with his stamp albums. But on evenings when he was not inclined to face the huge reading volume of his official paper work, he also liked to write his name in the hundreds of books which were sent to him, designating where they should go, to Hyde Park or the White House. He had a librarian's pride in the bulk of his collections of books as well as the tons of papers, just as he liked to compare the volume of his mail with Herbert Hoover's.

He read, too, of course. How and when, it is difficult to understand. The simple fact was that he could not play golf, though before his legs shriveled he devoted at least as much time to it as Eisenhower, Taft, Wilson, and Harding. He could not talk all the time, though sometimes he gave visitors the impression that he could. He read—and those who like the word "deeply" will be pleased with the proof that it was not always for simple entertainment. He left the evidence in handwritten comment on the fly leaves. Of Charles A. Beard's *A Foreign Policy for America,* published in 1940, he wrote, "'40 years' hard & continuous study' has brought forth an inbred mouse." He thought Raymond Leslie Buell's *Isolated America,* published in the same year, amounted to "the theorisms of an academician who has never shouldered public responsibilities." He decided that Alexander P. de Seversky's *Victory through Air Power* showed him to be a man who "knows planes but not military aviation." He called one of John T. Flynn's angry books about him "rather dull fiction." He might have surprised some of his critics by his comment on a book called *The Road to Plenty,* that it was "too good to be true—you can't get something for nothing." He noted that George Bernard Shaw's *The Intelligent Woman's Guide to Socialism and Capitalism* was "words and more words."

He did not read, however, merely to make a record on fly leaves. Indeed, I suspect that he left no tracks or records where he read the most. Perhaps the best guide to the books which he read as Roosevelt and not as President is given in a letter written by Archibald MacLeish, the librarian of Congress, to Alexander Woollcott in June, 1940. That was the month in which France fell. It was the month in which in connection with defense the President urged the enactment of a steeply graduated excess profits tax. It was the month in which he angrily interpolated into a speech in Jefferson's Virginia his declaration that Mussolini's Italy which held the dagger "had struck it into the back of its neighbor." Obviously it was a serious time. It was then that MacLeish asked Woollcott to serve as an honorary consultant to the Library of Congress with his only duty to "maintain for the President in the White House a shelf of the very best mystery, detective, etc., stuff." Woollcott promptly wrote:

I accept my post as consultant and venture to enquire:

(a) How long is a shelf?

(b) May it, as I would suggest, include non-fiction works in the field of murder?

(c) Have you the means to assemble out-of-print items?

(d) I shall include some of the Simenon detective stories in their French texts, as these will delight the present incumbent and probably embarrass his successor.

Mr. Woollcott apparently was not reflecting upon any particular embarrassed successor. John Nance Garner was vice-president. Some Texans read, though they may see the need of no other language except Texan. Henry Wallace had been nominated to succeed him. Perhaps his political disaster grew from the fact that he could read—and write. And the Republican candidate was Wendell Willkie, who acquired a literary reputation as abruptly as he did a political one. The reading habits of none of them is under examination here.

Roosevelt read out of curiosity and for fun. The most important thing about Roosevelt and books, however, was the manner in which he institutionalized the function of the president as bookman-in-chief. Few things interested him more than the Hyde Park Library project, but that is largely a matter of papers, source material, etc., though he estimated that his books would just about equal the number Jefferson's library contained. (On the basis of the inflation of the printed word in our times, that seems to me still to leave Jefferson much the leader.)

More important than any of the items he collected, however, seem to me the men he assembled to give reality to the institution of the presidency as book chief of the Republic. Obviously, Roosevelt did not have much time in which to browse in Livy or meander through the writings of Lord Macaulay. He would not privately have pretended to a scholar's knowledge of William Tyndale's translation of the Bible. What was important was that he set himself up as presidential bookman better than any previous president, with a staff qualified to keep him in contact with books and ideas in the whole range from Plato to Edward Lear. His appointment of MacLeish as librarian of Congress may not have pleased all the librarians. Also, I suspect he was dodging a certain public prejudice against poets when he first described MacLeish as "a writer and I think he has been connected with 'Fortune'." Whatever MacLeish may have done to the Library, he brought ideas and passion to the administration. And, not less important, he brought understanding and lively literary companionship to a president whose literary interests fortunately included not only politically effective references to Adam Smith and John Stuart Mill but contemporary, perhaps even ephemeral, poetry. MacLeish would have approved his efforts to liven such an ever-lengthening book as the Congressional Record with a poem about the present Ambassadress to Italy, Clare Booth Luce. It may be worth repeating now, though not all those who disinter old bones may care for the resurrection of old poems. It was by Howard Dietz and ran like this:

O Lovely Luce—O Comely Clare!
Do you remember—way back there—
Holding your lacquered nails aloft,
"The war we fight," you said, "is soft."

Time and courage had marched on, the poem continued, and also Clare had been elected to Congress; however,

While still responding to the toasts,
Remember this: that words are ghosts.

And when it's mealtime never stoop
To see the letters in the soup.
The ghosts may form like homing birds.
"My God," you'll cry, "I ate my words!"

Also, MacLeish brought Roosevelt into communication with David Mearns, who Mr. MacLeish feared in his searches for such presidential references as the Cherable Isles might come in time "to resemble the bearded gentleman with the frenzied eye at the beginning of a certain poem of Mr. Coleridge's." Fortunately, he has not. Mearns is still there, the librarian in America I think most beloved of all scholars, and available to any president capable of communication with him in the world of books.

MacLeish and Mearns were only two of those who staffed the institution of books and the presidency which Roosevelt made. Closer to him than anyone was a dry and delightful gentleman from Vermont named William D. Hassett, who only recently retired as a presidential secretary. Roosevelt was not indulging in hyperbole when he inscribed his photograph to Bill Hassett as "my Swift, my Buckle and my Roget." Indeed, a good deal of the hyperbole written to departing politicians as well as the richest references to men and ideas which are expected regularly from a president were produced by Hassett himself. Hassett's duties included not only on occasion "drying the President's wash" as he described the laying out of documents for the signatures to dry, but also—as the President indicated—his work as attendant wit, historian, and dictionary. MacLeish and Mearns, Woollcott and Hassett, were only four of the voracious staffers of the President's literary curiosity and official requirements. There were also some of the early Brain Trusters. There was Samuel Eliot Morison, to whom he turned not only in his planning for the Hyde Park Library but in the writing of the history of the Navy and the war. There was, of course, Robert E. Sherwood, whose concerns spread naturally from *Abe Lincoln in Illinois* to Franklin Roosevelt in the White House in his time. The truth is that anybody and almost everybody might at various times serve on that staff. And there was also—never to be minimized—Eleanor Roosevelt.

In a very real sense she was the official representative of those people who think that presidents should be the first reader as well as the first citizen of the Republic. She put the right books by his bed. She brought authors to his dinner table. The list runs from Robert Benchley to Heywood Broun, from F. P. A. to Carl Sandburg. Mrs. Roosevelt was, according to one story, a little flabbergasted when after some insistence on her part Roosevelt took *Gone with the Wind* and completed it in one brief passage of reading in bed. The moral of the tale as told—the President's swift reading ability

—was emphasized by the fact that despite her incredulity he passed an informal examination which she gave him on characters, style, quality, and plot. Sometimes, however, Mrs. Roosevelt emphasized the almost tragic and comic proportions of the romantic ideas about presidents and the influence of the book on presidential power.

Certainly one of the most revealing books, not about presidential reading but about people's—and particularly authors' —ideas about presidential reading, was a brief, vivid, passionate, and utterly misapprehending little volume which Louis Adamic wrote before his death called *Dinner at the White House.* Mr. Adamic, like so many other Americans, had written a book containing ideas about democracy and the future —and also some final sharp words about the dangers of British imperialism after a war for the Four Freedoms. Mrs. Roosevelt praised the book in her column, "My Day." Adamic thanked her and got a sudden invitation to dinner at the White House in the second month of World War II. He and his wife set out in the natural excitement which attends an invitation to the presence of the presidency. They could not get hotel rooms in wartime Washington so they changed to long dress and black tie in the washrooms of the Washington Union Station. Their excitement seemed properly charged with even greater significance when at the small dinner Winston Churchill, whose presence was a secret, suddenly appeared in his plump person.

Mrs. Roosevelt told Adamic that she had given the book to the President, and Adamic quoted her, "The President gave his copy of your book to the Prime Minister and specially requested him to read it. And I did, too."

Obviously, Mr. Adamic concluded this was not a simple dinner party. He was not just an author though Roosevelt spoke to him about book sales—a sensitive subject with him. He never forgave Bennett Cerf of Random House because only 4,000 of 25,000 sets of his public papers were sold. The subject of book sales, Adamic reported, was quickly dropped. Talk passed on to more important things. According to Adamic all Churchill said about his book during the evening were two stuttering remarks, "I'm . . . I'm r-reading it" and "I . . . I . . . find it interesting." And he said he had read it "about . . . half way. D'you really think . . . there is a problem here?"

Adamic naturally thought there was. Roosevelt's total comment was to Mrs. Adamic "in a low serious voice." Adamic as eager eavesdropper quoted Roosevelt:

> "I read your husband's book. There's been a good deal of discussion of it around here, particularly as to which part is better, more valuable. Some people seem to like the first part best. But I like the last part. It has something. It has something," he repeated, gesturing with his hand as though shaping the thought and groping for the words which followed. "It opens vistas—it's an idea that really opens vistas." He gestured again but with a different motion—as if pushing out into unknown spaces. "It appeals to the imagination."
>
> "Will you tell that to your husband?" he said, the smile gone again. "Tell him that *I* like the *last* part of the book."

He was a great man for "vistas." That was the part which might have been the prod to Churchill. It was the part Churchill said he had not reached. So far as Adamic knew he never did. Mrs. Roosevelt in a few moments whisked the Adamics away from the Big Two to a Toscanini concert. Afterwards the Adamics took a night train to Philadelphia and on their way home stopped for early breakfast at a roadside eating joint.

"From White House to Toddle House," Stella Adamic said. It seemed funny as well as exciting then. It is a sad little story in retrospect. It served later to underscore Adamic's pessimism about postwar democratic progress. A little later, *Dinner at the White House* seemed less a description of a literary evening underscoring the power of the book in public affairs than a sort of explanation in advance of tragic Adamic's suicide. That certainly is not a funny story even if it included almost a self-burlesque of romantic attitudes about presidents—and prime ministers—and books and earnest authors, too.

Books and authors at the White House under any administration make a part of a strange procession. All kinds pour in. Perhaps even more than Franklin Roosevelt, Mrs. Roosevelt gave a special Rooseveltian quality to the congregation which has never been described better than in connection with her Uncle Theodore by Mr. Dooley—who I suspect was an author who really did influence presidents. He described a not entirely improbable company at a White House meal in TR's time. The guests included: "Oscar Featherstone, the champeen roller-skater of Harvard '98; Pro-fissor McGlue, th' archyologist, Lord Dum de Dum, Mike Kehoe, Immanuel Kant Gumbo, th'naygro pote, Horrible Hank, th' bad lands scout, Sinitor Lodge, Lucy Emerson Tick, th' writer on female sufferage, Mud-in-th'-Eye, th' chief iv th' Ogallas, Gin'ral Powell Clayton, th' Mexican mine expert, four rough riders with their spurs on, th' Ambassadure iv France an' th' Cinquovasti fam'ly, jugglers."

Tragically as it turned out, Adamic became a member of such a company. It was a coincidence that he joined it at a time when Churchill dropped in secretly from the air a month after Pearl Harbor. Of course, Churchill and Roosevelt should have been thinking about such things as the postwar elimination of imperialism, prejudice, and oppression. They should have been reading books about such subjects. Nothing seems quite so clear, however, from Adamic's own report as that they had other things than his book on their minds, things to talk about after the Adamics and Mrs. Roosevelt went off to the concert and Adamic could not hear the music of Toscanini for hearing in imagination FDR and Churchill engaged in great and sometimes acrimonious debate about his book. And as of that evening in January, 1942, I am prepared to forgive them whatever may have been the mistakes which might have been avoided if they had read Adamic's book. The certain fact is that Mrs. Roosevelt did read it and obviously she did not keep secret what it said. From her undoubtedly Roosevelt heard about the first part and the last part. I expect the "vistas" was his own idea. The clear fact is that presidents and prime ministers, and I suspect some college presidents and even professors, as time goes on have to learn to read with their ears.

I understand—I must get some librarian to check it for me—that Saint Augustine wrote *The City of God* while the Vandals were at the gates. Perhaps it would reassure us in our times if we had the feeling that presidents in the Cold War turned to such books for relaxation and stimulation. Perhaps they do. What we can best hope for I think is a man in the presidency aware of books and aware of them not only in solemnity but in liveliness and delight. Franklin Roosevelt was such a man. Perhaps he gave too much attention to bindings and editions. Sometimes undoubtedly the rare book appealed to him more than the inwardly rich one. Undoubtedly he gave more attention to Kipling than—who shall we say—Santayana. He preferred some doggerel to the beautifully dressed reaction of T. S. Eliot. Most important of all, it seems to me in terms of the security of the American people, he liked to read for fun. The man who reads only for improvement is beyond the hope of much improvement before he begins. So is the president. I am glad that FDR had Woollcott's shelf and not merely Dr. Eliot's five-foot shelf at hand. It seems to me wholly good when he was at his tired end that he reached for such a book as might have gone on that Woollcott shelf. There may be those who wish that he had called for Ecclesiastes—Gibbon—Shakespeare—Milton. The book he had been reading, however, the last night before he died was a paperback which might have been bought in any drugstore, except maybe such a one as N. J. Bartlett's in Boston once was said to be. It was called *The Punch and Judy Murders,* and it was marked at a chapter headed "Six Feet of Earth." Roosevelt's Negro valet—who, of course, was a part of his book staff, too—found it by his bed.

It was not a trivial item. No reader or president is to be more distrusted than the one who reads only the great books. That in itself marks a docility and a humorlessness dangerous in leadership. That does not mean that we respect those who read only trash. It does mean that the good reader seeks and finds—through the institution of the presidency, the library, or the drugstore—the books which meet his need in every hour first and last. And that the essential book, whether bound in vellum or cardboard, produced by a pulp writer or a philosopher, is the book which meets the need of a man. That is never so true as in the case of a president of the United States.

REFERENCES

BIBLIOGRAPHICAL NOTE on JEFFERSON . . . *Bestor*

Indispensable to any study of Jefferson's handling of books is the *Catalogue of the Library of Thomas Jefferson,* compiled with annotations by E. Millicent Sowerby (Washington: Library of Congress, 1952–), to be completed in five volumes, of which three have appeared. Each book in the library that Jefferson sold to Congress in 1815 is described with full bibliographical detail, and in the annotations the compiler prints virtually every discoverable reference by Jefferson to the book in question. The majority of the quotations from Jefferson in the present paper are taken from this compilation, which is cited as *Catalogue,* ed. Sowerby.

The definitive edition of the *Papers of Thomas Jefferson,* edited by Julian P. Boyd (Princeton: Princeton Univ. Press, 1950-) is to be completed in fifty-two volumes, of which nine have appeared, covering the period through June, 1786. This edition is cited as *Papers,* ed. Boyd. Of the older editions, the *Writings of Thomas Jefferson,* edited by Paul Leicester Ford (10 vols., New York, 1892–99), presents the more accurate text, while the *Writings of Thomas Jefferson,* edited by Andrew A. Lipscomb and Albert E. Bergh (20 vols., Washington, 1903–05) is the more extensive. These are cited as *Writings,* ed. Ford, and *Writings,* ed. Lipscomb and Bergh, respectively.

The most extensive collection of manuscripts is in the Library of Congress, and these have been reproduced on 101 reels of microfilm, prints of which are in a number of libraries, including that of the University of Illinois. Documents from this collection are cited as Jefferson Papers, Library of Congress, with folio numbers.

The notes occasionally provide references to two sources for a given document. Quotations follow literally the text as given in the first citation, except that the initial letter of each sentence is capitalized, contrary to Jefferson's normal practice (a practice which some editors follow and others do not). Letters written above the line have been printed on the line, abbreviations being expanded by inserting the necessary letters in square brackets. Unless otherwise stated, Jefferson is to be understood as the writer of any letter cited in the notes.

Five book-lists constitute the principal contemporary records of Jefferson's activity as a collector and planner of libraries:

(i) A manuscript catalogue of his personal library, which Jefferson began in 1783 and in which he continued to record his acquisitions through 1814. This manuscript volume is in the Massachusetts Historical Society, and each entry is transcribed in its appropriate place in *Catalogue,* ed. Sowerby. A microfilm copy of the manuscript is in the University of Illinois Library.

(ii) *Catalogue of the Library of the United States. To Which Is Annexed, a Copious Index, Alphabetically Arranged* (Washington: Printed by Jonathan Elliot, 1815). This is a list of the books purchased from Jefferson, and was printed from a fair copy of No. i which has since disappeared. The catalogue departed, however, from Jefferson's own arrangement of titles.

(iii) "President Jefferson's Catalogue of Books for the University of Virginia Library, 1825," manuscript in the Alderman Library, University of Virginia; microfilm in University of Illinois Library. This 86-page manuscript lists 3,113 titles and bears the following notation at the end: "The preceding catalogue is that of the books with the purchase of which Mr. Wm. Hilliard is charged on behalf of the University of Virginia. June 3, 1825. Th. Jefferson, Rector."

(iv) *Catalogue of the Library of the University of Virginia. Arranged Alphabetically* (Charlottesville, Va.: Published by Gilmer, Davis, & Co., 1828), reprinted in a facsimile edition by the University of Virginia, 1945.

(v) *Catalogue. President Jefferson's Library. A Catalogue of the extensive and valuable Library of the late President Jefferson, (copied from the original MS., in his hand-writing, as arranged by himself,) to be sold at auction, at the Long Room, Pennsylvania Avenue, Washington City, by Nathaniel P. Poor, on the February, 1829* (Washington: Printed by Gales and

Seaton, 1829), microfilm (from copy in Library of Congress) in University of Illinois Library. The day of the month, the twenty-seventh, has been inserted in the blank space in many copies. A total of 931 titles are listed.

Several publications directly related to the subject of the present paper require mention: [Nathaniel F. Cabell, ed.], *Early History of the University of Virginia, As Contained in the Letters of Thomas Jefferson and Joseph C. Cabell* (Richmond, Va., 1856); Elizabeth Cometti (ed.), *Jefferson's Ideas on a University Library: Letters from the Founder of the University of Virginia to a Boston Bookseller* (Charlottesville, 1950); Library of Congress, *The Thomas Jefferson Bicentennial, 1743–1943: A Catalogue of the Exhibitions at the Library of Congress* (Washington, 1943); William L. Clements Library, *Thomas Jefferson, 1743–1943: A Guide to the Rare Books, Maps & Manuscripts Exhibited at the University of Michigan* (Ann Arbor, 1943); Randolph G. Adams, "Thomas Jefferson, Librarian," in his *Three Americanists* (Philadelphia, 1939), pp. 69–96; William H. Peden, *Some Aspects of Jefferson Bibliography* (Lexington, Va.: Washington and Lee University, 1941); Constance E. Thurlow and Francis L. Berkeley, Jr., *The Jefferson Papers of the University of Virginia: A Calendar* (Charlottesville, 1950); Library of Congress, *A Guide to Manuscript Materials Relating to the History of the Library of Congress,* compiled by Shirley Pearlove ([Washington, 1949]), mimeographed; James A. Servies, "Thomas Jefferson and His Bibliographic Classification" (unpublished master's thesis, University of Chicago, 1950), microfilm in the University of Illinois Library.

Biographies and general studies of Jefferson, and general histories of the Library of Congress and the University of Virginia, are cited when appropriate in the reference notes. Space precludes even a selective listing here.

REFERENCES

[1] A vivid account is in Henry Adams, *History of the United States* (New York, 1889–91), Book VIII, chaps. 5 and 6. See also Benson J. Lossing, *Pictorial Field-Book of the War of 1812* (New York, 1869),

pp. 932–36, which gives pictures of the Capitol before and after the fire.

[2] William D. Johnston, *History of the Library of Congress,* I (Washington, 1904), 65–68. One of the clerks, it interested me to discover, had been under the command of a Captain Bestor until furloughed on the Sunday preceding the destruction of the Capitol. *Annals of Congress,* 13th Cong., 3d sess., col. 954.

[3] The sources give conflicting accounts of the number of volumes that may have been saved. In a sample comparative check of the printed catalogues of 1812 and 1830, I failed to discover a single title that survived.

[4] To Thomas Cooper, Sept. 10, 1814. *Writings,* ed. Lipscomb and Bergh, XIV, 186.

[5] To James Madison, Sept. 24, 1814. *Writings,* ed. Lipscomb and Bergh, XIV, 196. The correspondence respecting the purchase is quoted at length in Johnston, *History of the Library of Congress,* I, 68–72, 80–84, 97–104, 141–49. As late as mid-January, 1814, Jefferson intended his library for the projected University of Virginia. To Thomas Cooper, Jan. 16, 1814. *Writings,* ed. Lipscomb and Bergh, XIV, 60.

[6] Speech of Cyrus King, Jan. 26, 1815, as quoted from the *National Intelligencer* by Johnston, *History of the Library of Congress,* I, 86. The speech was printed, with some verbal differences, in *Niles' Weekly Register,* VII, Supplement (1815), 63–65.

[7] To John Page, Feb. 21, 1770. *Papers,* ed. Boyd, I, 34. Books which Jefferson had purchased the preceding year are listed in an invoice from Perkins, Buchanan & Brown of London, Oct. 2, 1769. *Papers,* ed. Boyd, I, 34.

[8] "I thank you for making known to me Mr. Ticknor and Mr. Gray. . . . Mr. Ticknor is, particularly, the best bibliograph I have met with, and very kindly and opportunely offered me the means of reprocuring some part of the literary treasures which I have ceded to Congress, to replace the devastations of British vandalism at Washington. I cannot live without books. But fewer will suffice, where amusement, and not use, is the only future object. I am about sending him a catalogue, to which less than his critical knowledge of books would hardly be adequate." To John Adams, June 10, 1815. *Writings,* ed. Lipscomb and Bergh, XIV, 301–302. The last load of books for Congress left Monticello on May 8, 1815.

[9] *Catalogue. President Jefferson's Library . . . to be sold at auction* (1829), listing 931 titles.

[10] "A Bill for Establishing a Public Library." *Papers,* ed. Boyd, II, 544. This was bill No. 81 in the *Report of the Committee of Revisors,*

presented June 18, 1779. Though the bill was brought up in 1785 and 1786, it was never passed.

[11] See Johnston, *History of the Library of Congress,* I, 35–38.

[12] "President Jefferson's Catalogue of Books for the University of Virginia Library, 1825," manuscript, more fully described above.

[13] Jefferson's descriptive list, sent to George Wythe, Jan. 12, 1796. *Catalogue,* ed. Sowerby, II, 237. The account of Jefferson's collection of the laws of Virginia occupies pp. 236–65 of this volume of Miss Sowerby's *Catalogue.*

[14] List sent to George Wythe, Jan. 12, 1796. *Catalogue,* ed. Sowerby, II, 242.

[15] To George Wythe, Jan. 16, 1796. *Writings,* ed. Ford, VII, 52–55.

[16] The story is fully told in the correspondence assembled in *Catalogue,* ed. Sowerby, II, 255-61. The quotation is from Hening's letter of Dec. 26, 1806, on page 256.

[17] Thomas Jefferson, *Reports of Cases Determined in the General Court of Virginia. From 1730, to 1740; and from 1768, to 1772* (Charlottesville, 1829), p. v. The volume was edited and published by Thomas Jefferson Randolph.

[18] See the description of Jefferson's set of Diodorus Siculus, in *Catalogue,* ed. Sowerby, I, 18: "The Basel edition [1539], in quarto, is the first edition of the Greek text [edited by Vincent Obsopoeus], and has been cut down by Jefferson to resemble a duodecimo; and conflated with the octavo edition which is the Latin translation by [Laurent] Rhodomann [(Hanau, 1611)]. The whole is bound in four small volumes, of which the first is now lost. Notes on the fly-leaves of vol. II and III signed by F. Vinton, and made after the loss of vol. I, give a full explanation of Jefferson's procedure." The manuscript notes by Vinton read as follows: "Note. This is the editio princeps of Diodorus published in 4.° but here made to appear 12° by cutting of the margin. Mr. Jefferson interleaved it with the corresponding books of Laurent Rhodoman's latin version published at Hanau, by Wechel. 8.° 1611. F. Vinton." "Note. The first portion of this version, with the title page are lost. Mr. Jefferson intercalated books XVI–XX with the editio princeps of the Greek text of those books making 2 v. and having the preceding portion of the translation so far as he possessed it, bound as V. II. F. Vinton." Photostats in University of Illinois Library. Jefferson sometimes made composite texts in more than two languages. A trilingual set of Tacitus is described in *Catalogue,* ed. Sowerby, I, 38–39. The following sequence of leaves at the beginning of the first volume will indicate Jefferson's method of arrangement: (1) Latin title page, (2) Latin half-title, (3) Spanish title page, (4) Latin pages 3–4, (5) Spanish pages 1–2, (6) English pages 1–2, (7)

Latin pages 5–6, (8) Spanish pages 3–4, (9) English pages 3–4, (10) Latin pages 7–8, (11) English pages 5–6, (12) Latin pages 9–10, (13) Spanish pages 5–6, (14) English pages 7–8, (15) Latin pages 11–12, etc. Microfilm in University of Illinois Library. For other composite volumes see *Catalogue*, ed. Sowerby, I, 25, 29, 32, 37, 40, 41, 50; II, 29, 31, 32, 34, 38, 104.

Jefferson greatly disliked large and bulky volumes. "I have such a repugnance to the handling of 4tos & folios," he wrote one bookseller, "that I always prefer waiting for the 8vo. or smaller editions." To Joseph Milligan, Feb. 28, 1810. *Catalogue*, ed. Sowerby, I, 11; see also I, 26, 27, 493; and II, 97. One of Jefferson's sets included a volume of maps and plates which he cut down and folded to octavo size. *Catalogue*, ed. Sowerby, I, 20.

[19] See, for example, Jefferson's discussion of English, Latin, and Greek renderings of the psalms, in his letter to John Adams, Oct. 13, 1813. *Writings*, ed. Lipscomb and Bergh, XIII, 392–93.

[20] *Catalogue*, ed. Sowerby, I, 116–17, 181–82. Jefferson rushed the books off for binding just before his library was transferred to Congress, and he displayed them to visitors "with a satisfaction somewhat inconsistent with the measured gravity he claims in relation to such subjects generally." George Ticknor to E. Ticknor, Feb. 7, 1815, reprinted in Francis C. Rosenberger, *Jefferson Reader* (New York, 1953), p. 83, and quoted in *Catalogue*, ed. Sowerby, I, 182. Earlier Jefferson had thought these books "might be published as a Supplement to M. de Buffon, under the title of the 'Natural history of kings & Princes', or as a separate work & called 'Medicine for Monarchists'." To Madame de Tessé, Dec. 8, 1813. *Catalogue*, ed. Sowerby, I, 117.

[21] See Johnston, *History of the Library of Congress*, I, 141–47, 521, and plate 29 (following p. 521); see also James A. Servies, "Thomas Jefferson and His Bibliographic Classification," *passim.*

[22] To George Watterston, May 7, 1815. Johnston, *History of the Library of Congress*, I, 144.

[23] Jefferson modified his classification scheme to some degree in successive applications of it. Two elaborate tables present the earliest and the latest forms: (*A*) The table printed in *Catalogue of the Library of the United States* (1815), preliminary pp. [6–7], which follows the manuscript table prefixed to the catalogue that Jefferson kept from 1783 to 1814. Both are given in facsimile in *Catalogue*, ed. Sowerby, Vol. I, plates following p. xv. (*B*) The table printed in *Catalogue. President Jefferson's Library . . . to be sold at auction* (1829), p. 2.

The first of the three major divisions, "History," consisted of two subdivisions, "Civil" and "Natural." In version *A* "Civil History" was subdivided into "Civil Proper" and "Ecclesiastical," but in version *B* the latter was dropped completely. In both versions the subdivision

"Natural History" contained chapters for agriculture, chemistry, surgery, medicine, anatomy, zoology, botany, mineralogy, and technical arts. But Jefferson's original attempt to assign certain sciences to the division "Philosophy" apparently did not satisfy him. In version *A* there was a category "Physico-Mathematical" in the second division ("Philosophy"), and this comprised (among others) chapters on mechanics, statics, astronomy, and geography. In version *B* this category was abandoned, and the various sciences included in it were transferred to the first division ("History"). On the other hand, "Mathematics" remained in the second division ("Philosophy") in both versions.

[24] Jefferson allowed two subdivisions to "Philosophy," namely "Mathematical" and "Moral" or "Ethical." Under the latter he included not merely ethics but also religion, law, and politics. At the end of his life, Jefferson was facing the fact that a strictly materialistic point of view would require mind to be considered a part of natural history. In a letter to Augustus B. Woodward, March 24, 1824, he toyed with the idea of treating "ideology or mind" as a branch of zoology for purposes of classification, on the ground that "the faculty of thought belongs to animal history, is an important portion of it, and should there find its place." Dimly realizing, perhaps, how completely this would wreck his whole scheme of organizing knowledge, Jefferson concluded: "But these are speculations in which I do not now permit myself to labor." *Writings*, ed. Lipscomb and Bergh, XVI, 19.

[25] The third division, "Fine Arts," was, in contrast to the other divisions, a rather mechanical listing of the distinctive arts (architecture, music, etc.), and, so far as literature was concerned, a thoroughly conventional catalogue of literary forms (epic, romance, pastorals, odes, elegies, didactic, etc.).

[26] Point 9 in Jefferson's "An Explanation of the Views on Which This Catalogue Has Been Prepared," prefaced to "A Catalogue of Books Forming the Body of a Library for the University of Virginia," *circa* 1820–25, manuscript formerly in University of Virginia Library, but since destroyed. Printed in Johnston, *History of the Library of Congress*, I, 142–43; and in Saul K. Padover (ed.) *The Complete Jefferson* (New York, 1943), pp. 1091–92.

[27] *Ibid.*, point 1.

[28] Jefferson, *Notes on Virginia*, Query XVII. *Writings*, ed. Ford, III, 264.

[29] To N. G. Dufief, April 19, 1814. *Writings*, ed. Lipscomb and Bergh, XIV, 127.

[30] To John Tyler, June 28, 1804. *Writings*, ed. Lipscomb and Bergh, XI, 33.

[31] The *Notes on the State of Virginia,* written in 1781, were enlarged in 1782–83 and circulated in manuscript. After Jefferson went to Paris he had them privately printed, with a title page dated 1782, and he distributed copies to his friends in the spring of 1785. To forestall a pirated edition he agreed to their publication in French in 1786 and in English in 1787. See *Writings,* ed. Ford, III, 68–84; *Papers,* ed. Boyd, VIII, xxviii, 147–48, and plate facing p. 246; see also the publications cited in Boyd's notes.

[32] The extent of Jefferson's co-operation with contemporary historians is fully revealed in the excerpts from his correspondence compiled in Chapter IV, "Modern History—American," in *Catalogue,* ed. Sowerby, I, 196–285.

[33] To François Soulés, Jan. 19, 1787. *Catalogue,* ed. Sowerby, I, 223.

[34] To William Gordon, July 16, 1788. *Catalogue,* ed. Sowerby, I, 228. Jefferson wrote McLeod with a lower-case *l,* thus: M^{c}leod.

[35] To John Carey, Nov. 10, 1796. *Catalogue,* ed. Sowerby, I, 239.

[36] To Mathew Carey, June 19, 1813. *Catalogue,* ed. Sowerby, I, 262; *Writings,* ed. Lipscomb and Bergh, XIII, 264 (where the recipient is incorrectly given as Matthew Carr).

[37] To Benjamin Rush, Sept. 23, 1800. *Writings,* ed. Ford, VII, 460.

[38] Schenck *v.* U.S., 249 U.S. 47, at 52 (March 3, 1919).

[39] Jefferson, "First Inaugural Address," March 4, 1801. *Writings,* ed. Lipscomb and Bergh, III, 319.

[40] To Thomas Mann Randolph, May 30, 1790. *Catalogue,* ed. Sowerby, III, 2.

[41] *The Commonplace Book of Thomas Jefferson: A Repertory of His Ideas on Government,* ed. Gilbert Chinard ("Johns Hopkins Studies in Romance Literatures and Languages," Extra Vol. II; Baltimore, 1926), pp. 257–96; see also, in the introduction, Chinard's dating of the manuscript and his discussion of Jefferson's changing attitude toward Montesquieu. In 1769, just before the burning of his first library at Shadwell, Jefferson had acquired a set of Montesquieu. *Papers,* ed. Boyd, I, 34.

[42] To William Duane, Aug. 12, 1810. *Catalogue,* ed. Sowerby, III, 2; also printed p. 4. See also letter to Nathaniel Niles, March 22, 1801. *Writings,* ed. Ford, VIII, 24.

[43] To Duane, Aug. 12, Sept. 16, Oct. 25, and Nov. 13, 1810; Jan. 18, Jan. 26, March 28, and July 25, 1811; April 4, 1813; to Antoine L. C. Destutt de Tracy, Jan. 26, 1811; Nov. 28, 1813. *Catalogue,* ed. Sowerby, III, 4–9.

[44] To Pierre S. Dupont de Nemours, Nov. 29, 1813. A similar phrase occurs in the letters to Thomas Cooper, July 10, 1812, and Jan. 16,

1814; and to Samuel R. Demaree, Jan. 12, 1813. *Catalogue,* ed. Sowerby, III, 10–11. For Jefferson's discussions of Destutt de Tracy's commentary on Montesquieu, see (in addition to the letters excerpted by Sowerby): To Joseph C. Cabell, Feb. 2, 1816; to John Adams, Oct. 14, 1816; to Lafayette, May 17, 1816; to Joseph Milligan, Oct. 25, 1818. *Writings,* ed. Lipscomb and Bergh, XIV, 419; XV, 75; XIX, 237–39; XIX, 263–64.

[45] To William Duane, Jan. 22, 1813. *Writings,* ed. Lipscomb and Bergh, XIII, 213–14. To Destutt de Tracy, Nov. 28, 1813; to Dupont de Nemours, Feb. 28, 1815. *Catalogue,* ed. Sowerby, III, 9–10.

[46] University of Virginia, *Catalogue of the Library* (1828), p. 73.

[47] Thomas P. Peardon, *The Transition in English Historical Writing, 1760–1830* ("Columbia University Studies in History, Economics and Public Law," No. 390; New York, 1933), p. 19.

[48] To Mathew Carey, Nov. 22, 1818. *Catalogue,* ed. Sowerby, I, 176–78.

[49] *Ibid.*

[50] To William Duane, Aug. 12, 1810. *Catalogue,* ed. Sowerby, I, 157; *Writings,* ed. Lipscomb and Bergh, XII, 404–409.

[51] To Mathew Carey, Nov. 22, 1818. *Catalogue,* ed. Sowerby, I, 177.

[52] To William Duane, Aug. 12, 1810. *Catalogue,* ed. Sowerby, I, 157. In addition to the excerpts in Sowerby, see Jefferson's comments on Hume in his letters to John Adams, Nov. 25, 1816; and to John Cartwright, June 5, 1824. *Writings,* ed. Lipscomb and Bergh, XV, 86–87; XVI, 44.

[53] To William Duane, Aug. 12, 1810. *Catalogue,* ed. Sowerby, I, 157.

[54] To Mathew Carey, Nov. 22, 1818. *Catalogue,* ed. Sowerby, I, 177.

[55] *Ibid.* By "McCaulay" Jefferson meant Mrs. Catharine Macaulay's *History of England* (9 vols., London, 1763–83), a copy of which was in his library. *Catalogue,* ed. Sowerby, I, 164–65. The other historians mentioned by Jefferson are discussed below.

[56] John Baxter, *A New and Impartial History of England, From the most Early Period of Genuine Historical Evidence to the Present Important and Alarming Crisis; a Period Pregnant with the Fate of Empires, Kingdoms, and States. . . . Including An History of the American War and Revolution. . . . Interspersed with Remarks, Observations, and Reflections: By which former Errors are corrected, Absurdities pointed out, fabulous Narrations expunged, Party Prejudices removed, and what has hitherto appeared obscure and doubtful authenticated from the most respectable Evidence* (London: Printed for the Proprietors; and Sold by H. D. Symonds . . . , n.d., [*circa* 1796]). Microfilm copy in University of Illinois Library, from original volume in

New York Public Library. The complete title runs to 30 lines and the statement of authorship (quoted below) to 4 lines. This copy comprises 830 numbered pages, followed by a 4-page list of subscribers. The latest events treated are those of 1796, many of the engraved plates are of this date, and Miss Sowerby notes that the paper in the unspecified copy she examined was watermarked 1794, 1795, 1796; this would seem to fix the date of publication as 1796. In a letter describing the book Jefferson remarked that Baxter had "continued the history, but very summarily, to 1801" and that "the whole work is of 834. quarto pages." To William Duane, Aug. 12, 1810. *Catalogue,* ed. Sowerby, I, 176. On the basis of this statement Miss Sowerby conjectures that "Jefferson's copy had two more leaves, paged 831–834, and carried the history to 1801." *Ibid.,* I, 175. I see no reason for such a conjecture. Jefferson probably included the list of subscribers in his statement of the pagination. It is more probable that Jefferson mistook the terminal date than that a new edition, containing a 4-page supplement (quite inadequate for the five years supposedly covered) was published and has vanished without a trace.

[57] To Mathew Carey, Nov. 22, 1818. *Catalogue,* ed. Sowerby, I, 177. Jefferson described Baxter's procedure in almost identical terms in letters extending over nearly twenty years. To John Norvell, June 11, 1807; to William Duane, Aug. 12, and Sept. 16, 1810; to George Washington Lewis, Oct. 25, 1825. *Catalogue,* ed. Sowerby, I, 175–76. See also Francis C. Gray, *Thomas Jefferson in 1814,* reprinted in F. C. Rosenberger (ed.), *Jefferson Reader,* p. 79.

[58] Baxter, *New and Impartial History,* title page, Miss Sowerby correctly notes that "there is no suggestion from Baxter that his work is an adaptation or abridgment of Hume's History." *Catalogue,* I, 179.

[59] To William Duane, Aug. 12, 1810. *Catalogue,* ed. Sowerby, I, 176.

[60] To Duane, Aug. 12, and Sept. 16, 1810; to Carey, Nov. 22, 1818; to White, Feb. 5, 1820; Dec. 11, 1823; Jan. 7, 1824. *Catalogue,* ed. Sowerby, I, 175–79.

[61] *Catalogue,* ed. Sowerby, I, 175, 178–79.

[62] University of Virginia, *Catalogue of the Library* (1828); if present the book would have been listed on p. 13 or p. 111.

[63] Francis C. Gray, *Thomas Jefferson in 1814,* quoted in Rosenberger, *Jefferson Reader,* p. 79, and in *Catalogue,* ed. Sowerby, I, 156.

[64] To George Washington Lewis, Oct. 25, 1825. *Catalogue,* ed Sowerby, I, 156, 175 (excerpts only); *Writings,* ed. Lipscomb and Bergh, XVI, 124–29 (complete, but printed without the addressee's name). In this letter Jefferson still suggested Baxter, but merely as an introductory work for those "who shrink from the volume of Rapin," not as a substitute for Hume. The work of Rapin, in French, was in

Jefferson's library when it was sold to Congress. *Catalogue,* ed. Sowerby, I, 156. The English edition was in the University of Virginia Library when it opened. *Catalogue of the Library,* p. 18. Ludlow, Fox, and Belsham were in both libraries. *Catalogue,* ed. Sowerby, I, 154–55, 159, 180; University of Virginia, *Catalogue of the Library,* pp. 16, 15, 13. Brodie (published in 1822) was in the University Library only. *Ibid.,* p. 14.

[65] *Catalogue,* ed. Sowerby, II, 228–29. Jefferson's copy, now in the Library of Congress, was of the fourth edition (Oxford, 1770).

[66] To John Tyler, June 17, 1812. *Catalogue,* ed. Sowerby, II, 229. The derogatory phrase "Blackstone lawyers" also occurs in a letter to Thomas Cooper, Jan. 16, 1814. *Writings,* ed. Lipscomb and Bergh, XIV, 63.

[67] To Horatio G. Spafford, March 17, 1814. *Catalogue,* ed. Sowerby, II, 229.

[68] To James Madison, Feb. 17, 1826. *Writings,* ed. Ford, X, 376. Jefferson's allusion to Lord Chief Justice Mansfield (1705–93) is more fully explained in the excerpt quoted in footnote 72 below.

[69] To John Tyler, June 17, 1812. *Catalogue,* ed. Sowerby, II, 229.

[70] To Skelton Jones, July 28, 1809. *Catalogue,* ed. Sowerby, II, 262.

[71] To Bernard Moore, copy sent to John Minor, Aug. 30, 1814. *Catalogue,* ed. Sowerby, II, 218. Concerning this letter see footnote 73 below.

[72] "Begin with Coke's 4. institutes. These give a compleat body of the law as it stood in the reign of the 1st James, an epoch the more interesting to us, as we separated at that point from English legislation, and acknoledge [*sic*] no subsequent statutory alterations." To Dabney Terrell, Feb. 26, 1821. *Catalogue,* ed. Sowerby, II, 218. "The state of the English law at the date of our emigration, constituted the system adopted here. We may doubt, therefore, the propriety of quoting in our courts English authorities subsequent to that adoption; still more, the admission of authorities posterior to the Declaration of Independence, or rather to the accession of that King, whose reign, *ab initio,* was the very tissue of wrongs which rendered the Declaration at length necessary. . . . This relation to the beginning of his reign, would add the advantage of getting us rid of all Mansfield's innovations, or civilizations of the common law." By "civilization," Jefferson meant, of course, Mansfield's borrowings from the Roman or civil law, which Jefferson felt could not be amalgamated with the common law, even though he was himself ready to "admit the superiority of the civil over the common law code, as a system of perfect justice." To John Tyler, June 17, 1812. *Writings,* ed. Lipscomb and Bergh, XIII, 165–

66. See also the important discussion of Mansfield and Blackstone in Jefferson's letter to Philip Mazzei, Nov. 1785. *Papers*, ed. Boyd, IX, 71.

[73] To Dabney Terrell, Feb. 26, 1821. *Writings*, ed. Lipscomb and Bergh, XV, 318–22. To John Garland Jefferson, June 11, 1790. *Writings*, ed. Ford, V, 181. To John Minor, Aug. 30, 1814, and enclosed copy of letter to Bernard Moore. *Writings*, ed. Ford, IX, 480–85. The enclosed letter to Moore "was written near 50. years ago for the use of a young friend whose course of reading was confided to me," Jefferson explained. "I shall give it to you without change, except as to the books recommended to be read; later publications enabling me in some of the departments of science to substitute better, for the less perfect publications which we then possessed." The recent titles and editions are so numerous that the original text can hardly be conjectured; the letter must be regarded as essentially a statement of Jefferson's views in 1814. His recollection of the original date of writing was at fault, for the year 1764 (when Jefferson was only twenty-one) is undoubtedly too early.

[74] To John Tyler, May 26, 1810. *Catalogue*, ed. Sowerby, II, 228.

[75] See Jefferson, "An Essay towards Facilitating Instruction in the Anglo-Saxon," and especially the introductory letter to Herbert Croft, Oct. 30, 1798. *Writings*, ed. Lipscomb and Bergh, XVIII, 363. See also "Report of the Commissioners Appointed to Fix the Site of the University of Virginia," Aug. 4, 1818 (the so-called "Rockfish Gap Report," written by Jefferson). Roy J. Honeywell, *Educational Work of Thomas Jefferson* (Cambridge, 1931), p. 255.

[76] To Thomas Cooper, Jan. 16, 1814. *Catalogue*, ed. Sowerby, II, 212–13, 229; *Writings*, ed. Lipscomb and Bergh, XIV, 54–63.

[77] *Ibid.*

[78] *Ibid.*

[79] The texts of the resolution and the letters relating to it are printed in full in the appendix, pp. 39–44 above.

[80] Herbert B. Adams, *Thomas Jefferson and the University of Virginia* (U.S. Bureau of Education, Circular of Information, 1888, No. 1; Washington, 1888), p. 139.

[81] Philip A. Bruce, *History of the University of Virginia, 1819–1919* (5 vols., New York, 1920–22), I, 328–29. A similar objection is voiced by Gordon E. Baker, "Thomas Jefferson on Academic Freedom," American Association of University Professors *Bulletin*, XXXIX (Autumn, 1953), 377–87. On the other hand, the resolution is defended by Adrienne Koch, *Jefferson and Madison: The Great Collaboration* (New York, 1950), pp. 275–79. Her argument, however, overlooks the subtle but important difference (which I have tried in subsequent pages to point out) between establishing a *positive* stand-

ard of loyalty and *proscribing* antithetical ideas. She reads the latter policy into the resolution. Jefferson and Madison, she says, "were *unwilling to allow the entry* of political doctrines contradictory to the cherished freedoms of democratic society and Republican ideology. . . . The essential limits on freedom, Jefferson saw, included *uncompromising opposition* to systems of thought that would, if made effective, undermine that freedom. . . . Only the most romantic or sentimental liberals would be willing to jeopardize such gains by welcoming the very doctrines that proclaimed the end of human liberty." *Ibid.*, pp. 275, 278 (italics added). The second of the phrases I have italicized represents Jefferson's point of view; the first, in my judgment, does not. The assumption that the first position follows necessarily from the second is precisely the argument that Jefferson seems to me to have consistently rejected.

[82] To James Madison, Feb. 1, 1825. See also letter to Joseph C. Cabell, Feb. 3, 1825. Both are printed in the appendix.

[83] James Madison to Jefferson, Feb. 8, 1825. Printed in appendix.

[84] The texts are printed in *Writings of James Madison,* ed. Gaillard Hunt (9 vols., New York, 1900–1910), VI, 326–406.

[85] The text of Jefferson's first draft can only be conjectured from the correspondence, which is given in full in the appendix. In all probability the final resolution incorporates, almost unchanged, Jefferson's original version of the first paragraph and the first sentence of the second paragraph ("Whereas . . . generally approved by our fellow-citizens of this, and of the US."). The balance of the resolution follows closely the text suggested by Madison in the "Sketch" appended to his letter to Jefferson of Feb. 8, 1825. Quite possibly, however, Madison incorporated Jefferson's original characterizations of the various documents, for similar characterizations are to be found in the first sentence of the second paragraph of the resolution, applied to Locke and Sidney. Madison added to the list of documents "The Inaugural Speech and Farewell Address of President Washington." Jefferson accepted the suggestion, referring to "Gen[era]l Wash[ington]'s addresses" in the plural (to Madison, Feb. 12, 1825). The final resolution as offered to the board by Jefferson eliminated, however, the inaugural and referred simply to "the Valedictory address of President Washington."

The really crucial change made by Madison was in what he called "the operative passage" of the resolution, by which he presumably meant the concluding clause. The only version of this is Madison's own: "and that in the branch of the School of law which is to treat on the subject of Gov[ernmen]t these shall be used as the text & documents of the School." Madison, "Sketch," appended to his letter to Jefferson, Feb. 8, 1825; incorporated in the resolution adopted on

March 4 with only the change of "Gov[ernmen]t" to read "Civil polity." The character of Jefferson's original "operative passage" can only be gathered from Madison's comment that his own version was designed "to relax the absoluteness of its injunction." Madison to Jefferson, Feb. 8, 1825.

[86] James Madison to Jefferson, Feb. 8, 1825, printed in appendix. It should be noted that in the original manuscript the phrase "tho the public right be very different in the two cases" is inserted between the lines, with a caret to indicate the place of insertion.

[87] The job that needs to be done is carefully outlined in *A National Program for the Publication of Historical Documents: A Report to the President by the National Historical Publications Commission* (Washington: Government Printing Office, 1954).

REFERENCES . . . *Mearns*

[1] Speech at Kalamazoo, Michigan, August 27, 1856. *Collected Works* (Rutgers University Press, 1953), II, 364.

[2] Third-person autobiography, June, 1860. *Collected Works*, IV, 62.

[3] Samuel Haycraft to William H. Herndon, Elizabeth Town, Hardin County, Ky., August [1865?]. Herndon-Weik Manuscripts, Library of Congress, f. 2266.

[4] Dennis Friend Hanks to William H. Herndon, Chicago, June 13, 1865. Herndon-Weik Manuscripts, Library of Congress, f. 2170.

[5] Albert J. Beveridge, *Abraham Lincoln: 1809–1858* (Boston: Houghton Mifflin, 1928), I, 16.

[6] Dennis Friend Hanks to William H. Herndon, Chicago, June 13, 1865. Herndon-Weik Manuscripts, Library of Congress, f. 2170–71.

[7] A. H. Chapman to William H. Herndon, Charleston, Ill., September 8, 1865. Herndon-Weik Manuscripts, Library of Congress, f. 2295–96.

[8] Nat Grigsby to William H. Herndon, Gentryville, Ind., September 4, 1865. Herndon-Weik Manuscripts, Library of Congress, f. 2276–78.

[9] Address to the New Jersey Senate, at Trenton, N.J., February 21, 1861. *Collected Works*, IV, 235–36.

[10] Augustus H. Chapman to William H. Herndon, Charleston, Ill., September 8, 1865. Herndon-Weik Manuscripts, Library of Congress, f. 2294–96.

[11] See, for example, David Turnham's statement to William H. Herndon, September 15, 1865. Herndon-Weik Manuscripts, Library of Congress, f. 2353.

[12] Statement of Mrs. Matilda Johnston More to William H. Herndon, September 18, 1865. Herndon-Weik Manuscripts, Library of Congress, f. 2317.

[13] Sarah Bush Lincoln's statement to William H. Herndon, Charleston, Ill., September 8, 1865. Herndon-Weik Manuscripts, Library of Congress, f. 2312.

[14] Mentor Graham's statement to James Quay Howard, in David C. Mearns, *The Lincoln Papers* (Garden City, N.Y.: Doubleday, 1948), I, 156.

[15] N. W. Branson to William H. Herndon, Petersburg, Ill., August 3, 1865. Herndon-Weik Manuscripts, Library of Congress, f. 2272.

[16] R. B. Rutledge to William H. Herndon, Oskaloosa, Iowa, December 4, 1866. Herndon-Weik Manuscripts, Library of Congress, f. 2846–47.

[17] J. Rowan Herndon to William H. Herndon, Quincy, Ill., August 16, 1865. Herndon-Weik Manuscripts, Library of Congress, f. 2274–75. For other references to Mr. Lincoln's undignified posture, see David C. Mearns, *The Lincoln Papers,* I, 154; and William G. Greene to William H. Herndon, Tallula, Ill., November 27, 1865, Herndon-Weik Manuscripts, Library of Congress, f. 2392.

[18] J. Rowan Herndon to William H. Herndon, Quincy, Ill., August 16, 1865. Herndon-Weik Manuscripts, Library of Congress, f. 2274.

[19] Abner Y. Ellis to William H. Herndon, Moro, Madison County, Ill., December 11, 1866. Herndon-Weik Manuscripts, Library of Congress, f. 2888.

[20] Abner Y. Ellis to William H. Herndon, Moro, Madison County, Ill., December 6, 1866. Herndon-Weik Manuscripts, Library of Congress, f. 2854.

[21] Mentor Graham to William H. Herndon, Petersburg, Ill., July 15, 1865. Herndon-Weik Manuscripts, Library of Congress, f. 2237.

[22] R. B. Rutledge to William H. Herndon, n.p., n.d. Herndon-Weik Manuscripts, Library of Congress, f. 2930.

[23] Third-person autobiography, June, 1860. David C. Mearns, *The Lincoln Papers,* I, 143; and *Collected Works,* IV, 62.

[24] David C. Mearns, *The Lincoln Papers,* I, 152–53.

[25] William G. Greene to William H. Herndon, Elm Wood, Ill., May 30, 1865. Herndon-Weik Manuscripts, Library of Congress, f. 2139.

[26] David C. Mearns, *The Lincoln Papers,* I, 155.

[27] Mentor Graham to William H. Herndon, Petersburg, Ill., May 29, 1865. Herndon-Weik Manuscripts, Library of Congress, f. 2121–22.

[28] William G. Greene to William H. Herndon, June 7, 1865. Herndon-Weik Manuscripts, Library of Congress, f. 2154–55.

[29] David C. Mearns, *The Lincoln Papers,* I, 156.

[30] Lynn McNulty Greene to William H. Herndon, Avon, Fulton County, Ill., July 30, 1865. Herndon-Weik Manuscripts, Library of Congress, f. 2260–63.

[31] Dr. Jason Duncan to William H. Herndon, n.p., n.d. Herndon-Weik Manuscripts, Library of Congress, f. 3864.

[32] R. B. Rutledge to William H. Herndon, n.p., n.d. Herndon-Weik Manuscripts, Library of Congress, f. 2930.

[33] David C. Mearns, *The Lincoln Papers,* I, 153.

[34] Third-person autobiography, June, 1860. *Collected Works,* IV, 65.

[35] Mentor Graham to William H. Herndon, Petersburg, Ill., May 29, 1865. Herndon-Weik Manuscripts, Library of Congress, f. 2119.

[36] David C. Mearns, *The Lincoln Papers,* I, 153.

[37] Dennis Friend Hanks to William H. Herndon, December 27, 1865. Herndon-Weik Manuscripts, Library of Congress, f. 2405.

[38] William H. Herndon and Jesse W. Weik, *Abraham Lincoln: The True Story of a Great Life* (New York: Appleton, 1892), I, 42.

[39] Lincoln Memorial Collection of Chicago, *Sketch of the Life of Abraham Lincoln and a Catalogue of Articles Once Owned and Used by Him . . . On Exhibition at the Exposition Building* [n.p., 1893?], pp. 24–25. See also Lincoln Memorial Collection of Chicago, *Catalogue of Articles Owned and Used By Abraham Lincoln* (1888) [pp. 4–5].

[40] Stan V. Henkels (comp.), *The Valuable Collection of Autographs and Historical Papers Collected by the Hon. Jas. T. Mitchell . . . Also the Entire Lincoln Memorial Collection, of Chicago, Ill. . . . To Be Sold Wednesday and Thursday, Dec. 5th and 6th, 1894 . . . At the Book Auction Rooms of Thos. Birch's Sons, Philada., Pa.,* p. 104.

[41] Ida Minerva Tarbell, *The Life of Abraham Lincoln* (New York: Lincoln History Society, 1924), I, 36 n.

[42] Third-person autobiography, June, 1860. David C. Mearns, *The Lincoln Papers,* I, 146–47.

[43] William Butler to James Quay Howard. David C. Mearns, *The Lincoln Papers,* I, 151–53.

[44] Henry McHenry to William H. Herndon, Petersburg, Ill., May 29, 1865. Herndon-Weik Manuscripts, Library of Congress, f. 2128–29.

[45] Lynn McNulty Greene to William H. Herndon, Avon, Fulton County, Ill., July 30, 1865. Herndon-Weik Manuscripts, Library of Congress, f. 2265.

[46] Jason Duncan to William H. Herndon, n.p., n.d. Herndon-Weik Manuscripts, Library of Congress, f. 3865.

[47] Henry McHenry to James Quay Howard. David C. Mearns, *The Lincoln Papers,* I, 158.

[48] Allan Jasper Conant, "My Acquaintance with Abraham Lincoln," in Authors Club, *Liber Scriptorum: The First Book of the Authors Club* (New York, 1893), p. 172.

[49] To John M. Brockman, September 25, 1860. *Collected Works,* IV, 121.

[50] William H. Herndon and Jesse W. Weik, *Abraham Lincoln: The True Story of a Great Life,* II, 6.

[51] To Isham Reavis, November 5, 1855. *Collected Works,* II, 327.

[52] Fragment: Notes for a Law Lecture [July 1, 1850?]. *Collected Works,* II, 81.

[53] Address Before the Young Men's Lyceum of Springfield, Ill., January 27, 1838. *Collected Works,* I, 112.

[54] Abner Y. Ellis to William H. Herndon, Moro, Madison County, Ill., December 11, 1866. Herndon-Weik Manuscripts, Library of Congress, f. 2888.

[55] William H. Herndon and Jesse W. Weik, *Abraham Lincoln: The True Story of a Great Life,* II, 188.

[56] William H. Herndon to Charles H. Hart, February 13, 1866. Quoted in William Harrison Lambert, *Library of the Late Major William H. Lambert . . . To Be Sold January 14, 15, and 16, 1914* (New York, Metropolitan Art Association [1914]), p. 17.

[57] Many of the books known once to have been in Lincoln's library are listed in a broadside: *By W. O. Davie & Co. At Book Sale Rooms, 16 East Fourth Street, Cincinnati. The Private Library! of W. H. Herndon, Esq. (former law partner of Hon. Abraham Lincoln), at auction on Friday and Saturday evenings, Jan. 10 and 11, 1873;* photostat in Library of Congress.

[58] Joseph Gillespie to William H. Herndon, Edwardsville, Ill., December 8, 1866. Herndon-Weik Manuscripts, Library of Congress, f. 2873.

[59] Milton Hay to John Hay, Springfield, February 8, 1887. Abraham Lincoln Association, *Bulletin,* No. 25, December, 1931, pp. 8–9.

[60] Interview with John T. Stuart, December 20, 1866. Herndon-Weik Manuscripts, Library of Congress, f. 2246.

[61] *Second Lecture on Discoveries and Inventions,* February 11, 1859. *Collected Works,* III, 360–63 *passim.*

[62] Address Before the Wisconsin State Agricultural Society, Milwaukee, Wis., September 30, 1859. *Collected Works,* III, 480–81.

[63] John Hay to William H. Herndon, Paris, France, September 5, 1866. Herndon-Weik Manuscripts, Library of Congress, f. 2632.

[64] To Mrs. L. H. Phipps, March 9, 1863. *Collected Works,* VI, 130.

[65] Harry Edward Pratt, *The Personal Finances of Abraham Lincoln* (Springfield, Ill.: The Abraham Lincoln Association, 1943), pp. 180–81. Ruth Painter Randall, *Mary Lincoln: Biography of a Marriage* (Boston: Little, Brown, 1953), p. 262.

[66] Noah Brooks, "Personal Recollections of Abraham Lincoln," in *Harper's New Monthly Magazine,* XXXI, No. 182 (July, 1865), 224.

[67] J. Rowan Herndon to William H. Herndon, Quincy, Ill., August 16, 1865. Herndon-Weik Manuscripts, Library of Congress, f. 2274.

[68] Interview with John T. Stuart, December 20, 1866. Herndon-Weik Manuscripts, Library of Congress, f. 2246.

[69] William H. Herndon and Jesse W. Weik, *Abraham Lincoln: The True Story of a Great Life,* II, 147.

[70] Joseph Gillespie to William H. Herndon, Edwardsville, Ill., December 8, 1866. Herndon-Weik Manuscripts, Library of Congress, f. 2873.

[71] Frederick Marryat, *Diary in America* (London: Longmans, 1839), I, 41.

[72] Speech to the Springfield Scott Club, August 26, 1852. *Collected Works,* II, 157.

[73] "S." [i.e., Charles Sumner], "The Death of George Livermore," in *Boston Daily Advertiser,* Saturday, September 2, 1865, p. 2.

[74] William H. Herndon and Jesse W. Weik, *Abraham Lincoln: The True Story of a Great Life,* II, 164–65.

[75] J. Rowan Herndon to William H. Herndon, Quincy, Ill., August 16, 1865. Herndon-Weik Manuscripts, Library of Congress, f. 2274.

[76] N. W. Branson to William H. Herndon, Petersburg, Ill., August 3, 1865. Herndon-Weik Manuscripts, Library of Congress, f. 2272.

[77] To George Robertson, November 20, 1862. *Collected Works,* V, 502.

[78] Speech to the Springfield Scott Club, August 26, 1852. *Collected Works,* II, 148.

[79] James Prior's *Life and Character of Edmund Burke* is listed as in Herndon's library, when it was sold at auction in 1873.

[80] Dennis Friend Hanks to William H. Herndon, December 27, 1865. Herndon-Weik Manuscripts, Library of Congress, f. 2405.

[81] Noah Brooks, "Personal Recollections of Abraham Lincoln," in *Harper's New Monthly Magazine,* XXXI, No. 182 (July, 1865), 229.

[82] See, for example, Fragments of a Tariff Discussion [December 1, 1847]. *Collected Works,* I, 411. Speech to the Springfield Scott Club, August 14, 1852. *Collected Works,* II, 141. Speech at Chicago, Ill., July 10, 1858. *Collected Works,* II, 501. Speech Before the Republican State Convention, Springfield, Ill., June 16, 1858. *Collected Works,* II, 461. Address Before the Young Men's Lyceum of Springfield, Ill., January 27, 1838. *Collected Works,* I, 115.

[83] Reply to Loyal Colored People of Baltimore, Upon Presentation of a Bible [now in the Fisk University Library], September 7, 1864. *Collected Works,* VII, 542.

[84] Temperance Address, February 22, 1842. *Collected Works,* I, 276. (The quote is from Isaac Watts, *Hymns and Spiritual Songs,* Book I, Hymn 88.)

[85] Ellis fixes the year as 1841. See A. Y. Ellis to William H. Herndon, Moro, Madison County, Ill., February 14, 1866. Herndon-Weik Manuscripts, Library of Congress, f. 2490.

[86] Noah Brooks, "Personal Recollections of Abraham Lincoln," in *Harper's New Monthly Magazine,* XXXI, No. 182 (July, 1865), 229.

[87] The set, inscribed, is in the Library of Congress.

[88] Third-person autobiography, June, 1860. *Collected Works,* IV, 62.

[89] Milton Hay to John Hay, Springfield, Ill., February 8, 1887. Abraham Lincoln Association, *Bulletin,* No. 25, December, 1931, p. 8.

[90] To Edwin M. Stanton, November 11, 1863. *Collected Works,* VII, 11.

[91] Talcott Williams, "Lincoln the Reader," in *The American Review of Reviews,* LXI, No. 2 (February, 1920), 196.

[92] *Second Lecture on Discoveries and Inventions,* February 11, 1859. The manuscript is now owned by Justin G. Turner, of Los Angeles, Cal. *Collected Works,* III, 357.

[93] Speech in the United States House of Representatives on Internal Improvements, June 20, 1848. *Collected Works,* I, 489.

[94] John Locke Scripps, *Life of Abraham Lincoln* ([Peoria, Ill.: M. L. Houser, *ca.* 1931]), p. 15.

[95] John Locke Scripps to Abraham Lincoln, Chicago, July 17, 1860. David C. Mearns, *The Lincoln Papers,* I, 266.

[96] John Locke Scripps to William H. Herndon, Chicago, June 24, 1865. Herndon-Weik Manuscripts, Library of Congress, f. 2208.

[97] Library of Congress. Borrowers' Ledger L, 114.

[98] F. B. Carpenter, *Six Months at the White House with Abraham Lincoln* (New York: Hurd, 1866), pp. 114–15.

[99] William H. Herndon and Jesse W. Weik, *Abraham Lincoln: The True Story of a Great Life,* I, 104.

[100] Abner Y. Ellis to William H. Herndon, Moro, Madison County, Ill., January 30, 1866. Herndon-Weik Manuscripts, Library of Congress, f. 2444–45.

[101] Abner Y. Ellis to William H. Herndon, Moro, Madison County, Ill., February 14, 1866. Herndon-Weik Manuscripts, Library of Congress, f. 2489.

[102] Abner Y. Ellis to William H. Herndon, Moro, Madison County, Ill., December 6, 1866. Herndon-Weik Manuscripts, Library of Congress, f. 2854.

[103] Abner Y. Ellis to William H. Herndon, Moro, Madison County, Ill., December 11, 1866. Herndon-Weik Manuscripts, Library of Congress, f. 2888.

[104] Interview with John T. Stuart, December 20, 1866. Herndon-Weik Manuscripts, Library of Congress, f. 2246.

[105] To Mary Speed, September 27, 1841. *Collected Works,* I, 260.

[106] Speech to the Springfield Scott Club, August 26, 1852. *Collected Works,* II, 149.

[107] William Dean Howells, *Life of Abraham Lincoln* (Springfield, Ill.: Abraham Lincoln Association, 1938), pp. 31–32.

[108] William G. Greene's statement to James Quay Howard. David C. Mearns, *The Lincoln Papers,* I, 154.

[109] William G. Greene to William H. Herndon, Elm Wood, Ill., May 30, 1865. Herndon-Weik Manuscripts, Library of Congress, f. 2147. See also Lynn McNulty Greene to William H. Herndon, Avon, Fulton County, Ill., July 30, 1865. Herndon-Weik Manuscripts, Library of Congress, f. 2263–64.

[110] William G. Greene to William H. Herndon, Tallula, Ill., November 27, 1865. Herndon-Weik Manuscripts, Library of Congress, f. 2392.

[111] Abner Y. Ellis to William H. Herndon, Moro, Madison County, Ill., January 30, 1866. Herndon-Weik Manuscripts, Library of Congress, f. 2444.

[112] William Dean Howells, *Life of Abraham Lincoln,* p. 31.

[113] Milton Hay to John Hay, Springfield, Ill., February 8, 1887. Abraham Lincoln Association, *Bulletin,* No. 25, December, 1931, p. 9.

[114] To James G. Wilson, May 2, 1860. *Collected Works,* IV, 48.

[115] Memorandum, January 25, 1865. *Collected Works,* VIII, 237.

[116] To James H. Hackett, August 17, 1863. *Collected Works,* VI, 392–93. The original of this letter is now owned by Alfred Whital Stern, of Chicago.

[117] Adolphe de Chambrun, *Impressions of Lincoln and the Civil War* (New York: Random House, 1952), p. 83.

[118] R. Gerald McMurtry, "Lincoln Knew Shakespeare," in the *Indiana Magazine of History,* XXXI, No. 4 (December, 1935), 267.

[119] Joshua F. Speed to William H. Herndon, Louisville, Ky., January 12, 1866. Herndon-Weik Manuscripts, Library of Congress, f. 2424.

[120] John Locke Scripps to William H. Herndon, Chicago, June 24, 1865. Herndon-Weik Manuscripts, Library of Congress, f. 2207.

[121] Speech to the Springfield Scott Club, August 14, 1852. *Collected Works,* II, 143.

[122] To James G. Wilson, May 2, 1860. *Collected Works,* IV, 48.

[123] Interview with John T. Stuart, December 20, 1866. Herndon-Weik Manuscripts, Library of Congress, f. 2246.

[124] Louis John Kolb, *Superlative Washington, Lincoln and Grant Autographs, Books and Relics . . . Collected by the late Col. Louis J. Kolb . . . To be sold by order of the executors . . . at unrestricted public auction, Monday, November 17, 1941* (Philadelphia: William D. Morley, Inc., 1941), p. 76.

[125] Henry Clay Whitney to William H. Herndon, Lawrence, Kan., December 30, 1866. Herndon-Weik Manuscripts, Library of Congress, f. 2921.

[126] William H. Herndon to Henry Clay Whitney, Springfield, Ill., January 12, 1867. O. W. Holmes Papers, Library of Congress.

[127] Francis B. Carpenter, *Six Months at the White House with Abraham Lincoln,* pp. 58–59. See also William H. Herndon and Jesse W. Weik, *Abraham Lincoln: The True Story of a Great Life,* I, 320.

[128] Noah Brooks, "Personal Recollections of Abraham Lincoln," in *Harper's New Monthly Magazine,* XXXI, No. 182 (July, 1865), 229.

[129] *Ibid.*

[130] *Ibid.*

[131] *Ibid.*

[132] To Andrew Johnston, April 18, 1846. *Collected Works,* I, 377.

[133] Interview with John T. Stuart, December 20, 1866. Herndon-Weik Manuscripts, Library of Congress, f. 2246.

[134] Frederic Lauriston Bullard, "Lincoln's Copy of Poe's Poems," in *The Abraham Lincoln Quarterly,* IV, No. 1 (March, 1946), 30–35. See also Lincoln's Address Before the Wisconsin State Agricultural Society, Milwaukee, Wis., September 30, 1859. *Collected Works,* III, 472.

[135] Francis B. Carpenter, *Six Months at the White House with Abraham Lincoln,* p. 115.

[136] To Andrew Johnston, April 18, 1846. *Collected Works,* I, 378.

[137] *Ibid.* See also Francis B. Carpenter, *Six Months at the White House with Abraham Lincoln,* pp. 58–60.

[138] Carpenter, *supra.*

[139] Francis B. Carpenter to William H. Herndon, New York, December 4, 1866. Herndon-Weik Manuscripts, Library of Congress, f. 2841.

[140] William H. Herndon, *Abraham Lincoln Miss Ann Rutledge New Salem Pioneering The Poem: A Lecture* (Springfield, Ill. [H. E. Barker], 1910), pp. 56, 64.

[141] William H. Herndon and Jesse W. Weik, *Abraham Lincoln: The True Story of a Great Life,* I, 131–32.

[142] William H. Herndon and Jesse W. Weik, *Herndon's Life of Lincoln, with Introduction and Notes by Paul M. Angle* (Cleveland: World Publishing Company, 1949), p. xli.

[143] Eulogy on Zachary Taylor, Chicago, July 25, 1850. *Collected Works,* II, 90–91.

[144] Francis B. Carpenter, *Six Months at the White House with Abraham Lincoln,* pp. 60–61.

[145] Photostat of the manuscript, in the Library of Congress.

[146] Noah Brooks, "Personal Recollections of Abraham Lincoln," in *Harper's New Monthly Magazine,* XXXI, No. 182 (July, 1865), 229.

[147] J. Rowan Herndon to William H. Herndon, Quincy, Ill., August 16, 1865. Herndon-Weik Manuscripts, Library of Congress, f. 2274–75.

[148] Augustus H. Chapman to William H. Herndon, Charleston, Ill., September 8, 1865. Herndon-Weik Manuscripts, Library of Congress, f. 2296.

[149] William Dean Howells, *Life of Abraham Lincoln,* p. 32.

[150] David C. Mearns, *The Lincoln Papers,* I, 150.

[151] William H. Herndon and Jesse W. Weik, *Herndon's Life of Lincoln, with Introduction and Notes by Paul M. Angle,* p. 293.

[152] William H. Herndon and Jesse W. Weik, *Abraham Lincoln: The True Story of a Great Life,* II, 1.

[153] Francis B. Carpenter, *Six Months at the White House with Abraham Lincoln,* p. 154.

[154] To William H. Herndon, December 12, 1847. *Collected Works,* I, 419.

[155] To Richard F. Bartlett, April 17, 1840. *Collected Works,* I, 209.

[156] To Richard S. Thomas, February 14, 1844. *Collected Works,* I, 332.

[157] Endorsement, January 6, 1857. *Collected Works,* II, 388.

[158] See, for example, his Speech at a Republican Banquet, Chicago, Ill., December 10, 1856; Letter to Henry L. Pierce and others, April 6, 1859; Speech at Manchester, N.H., March 1, 1860; Fragment on the Constitution and the Union, *circa* January, 1861; *Collected Works,* II, 383; III, 375; III, 551; IV, 168–69.

[159] William H. Herndon and Jesse W. Weik, *Abraham Lincoln: The True Story of a Great Life,* II, 165.

[160] *Ibid.,* II, 188.

[161] Cooper Institute Address, February 27, 1860. *Collected Works,* III, 541.

[162] William H. Herndon and Jesse W. Weik, *Abraham Lincoln: The True Story of a Great Life,* II, 65. Herndon misquotes Parker. It is transcribed accurately in the text of this paper.

[163] William H. Herndon, "The Analysis of Mr. Lincoln's Character," in Osborn H. Oldroyd, *The Lincoln Memorial: Album-Immortelles* (New York: Carleton, 1882), p. 533.